I0176582

We all have a community of interest.

Blogs
and Wikis

Blogs
and Wikis

TESOL Strategy Guide

DAVID KENT

Pedagogy Press

Copyright © 2017 David Kent.
All rights reserved.

No part of this publication may be reproduced, distributed, or transmitted in any
form or by any means, including photocopying, recording, or other electronic or
mechanical methods, without prior written permission, except in the case of brief
quotations embodied in critical reviews and certain other noncommercial uses
permitted by copyright law.

Distributable Content: The author and publisher grant permission for the copy
and distribution of handouts from this book for any and all instructional
purposes.

Trademark Notice: Product or corporate names may be trademarks or registered
trademarks, and are used only for identification and explanation without intent
to infringe.

Cover Photograph: © Can Stock Photo Inc. / fabian19

Although every precaution has been taken to verify the accuracy of the
information contained herein, the author and publisher assume no responsibility
for any errors or omissions. No liability is assumed for damages that may result
from the use of information contained within.

National Library of Australia Cataloguing-in-Publication entry:
Kent, David Bradley, author.
Blogs and wikis / David Kent.

ISBN: 9781925555110 (paperback) (6)
TESOL strategy guide ; 6.
Includes bibliographical references.
Teachers of English to Speakers of Other Languages.
Education technology.
Teaching—Aids and devices.
Teachers—Training of
Blogs.
Wikis (computer science).
English language—Study and teaching—Foreign speakers.

Pedagogy Press. Sydney, Australia.
www.pedagogypress.com

First Edition.

For teachers everywhere.

CONTENTS

Preface

This *TESOL Strategy Guide,* number six in the set, arose out of the clear need to provide teacher training and a means of professional development to educators living and working in the Republic of Korea. Many expatriate English language instructors have arrived in-country without training as a teacher or educator and are often left to take care of their own professional development while engaged in teaching English to speakers of other languages (TESOL). As many of these teachers come to enjoy working as expatriates, they often begin to seek out their own professional development on topics that they wish to learn more about, on skills that they wish to gain, and on techniques that they wish to integrate within their classrooms. It is this need, which is common to all teachers of English in all contexts around the globe, that this book seeks to fill.

Organization of the text

Each *TESOL Strategy Guide* can be read standalone or in conjunction with others from the set. Each book provides information on a technology topic, and has been designed around a question-based format similar to the following:

- Overview
- What is … ?
- How can I use … ?
- What types of … exist?
- What elements are behind an effective … ?
- How can … lend itself to TESOL?
- How can I start using … with students?
- How do I evaluate a … ?
- What tools are available for … creation?
- How do I craft a … ?
- How would I use a tool to create a … ?
- What are the key points behind … use in the TESOL context?

A comprehensive list of resources with links to pertinent web sites and applications is included, along with lesson plan guides, example implementation techniques, and various free to use handouts for the teacher and student alike. A reference list of all works cited also allows those teachers with an interest in a particular topic to engage in reading further on the issues that most interest them and impact their learners.

It is hoped that this book will provide both education and something new for all teachers – be they trained or untrained, pre-service, in-service, seasoned, or retired.

1

Overview

Blogs and wikis are different to other websites because they demand interaction. Blogs ask readers to think and respond to the various ideas, questions, and links that have been posted by the author or authors. Wikis demand interaction by inviting readers to contribute, edit, and author the content of the website. The emergence of blogs and wikis, as well as other user-generated content, has shifted the web from a place of 'static' information provision (Web 1.0) to one of 'dynamic' information sharing and user-generated content (Web 2.0), and it is these elements that lie at the heart of the social media movement. People blog so that their voices and thoughts can be heard, and they create and edit wikis so that their knowledge can be shared. Bloggers interact with readers by providing links within their posts, and by responding to reader comments on their posts. Meanwhile, there are three categories of people accessing a wiki: readers, writers, and editors, and a person could be either one, two, or all three of these.

2 | Blogs and wikis

Throughout this book, the manner in which blogs and wikis are developed is considered while taking into account their pedagogical promise when teaching English to speakers of other languages (TESOL). An overview of instructional strategies, tasks, and activities suitable for second-language learners of English when working with blogs and wikis is provided, along with the considerations necessary for applying these tools successfully in the classroom. Also included are tutorials, photocopiable checklists, handouts, and templates, evaluation techniques, and a comprehensive list of a wide variety of resources.

2

What are blogs and wikis?

Both blogs and wikis are a form of content management system (CMS), and they are similar in structure and logic with both providing asynchronous computer mediated communication (CMC) and operating through a web browser interface. A blog will contain articles that are usually written by a single author or blogger, and while visitors can add comments to the original blog post or entry, they are not able to change the originally posted content. A wiki, on the other hand, will contain a single piece of content that has potentially had multiple people working on it, with a single article having from one to perhaps ten or even hundreds of authors coming to form it. This editability and collaborative production are what differentiates blog posts from wiki articles. In either case, blog posts and wiki article edits, when they are made, are instantly visible to all other users.

Blogs

The term 'blog' was coined in 1999 (Merholz, 1999), and arose from splitting the term web log (coined in 1997) into 'we blog' (Wortham, 2007). Essentially, a blog is a web site where a user or a number of users post entries in journal style, and these appear in reverse chronological order. Writing to and updating a blog is easy and can be done from any web browser.

The first blogs were mainly journal or diary-based entries about a person and their day-to-day activities and thoughts. These days, blogs cover almost any topic imaginable, from those bloggers that talk about themselves and their daily lives, through to others who mention nothing about themselves but post articles that provide tips, technical information, scandals and rumors, or specific advice regarding their interests. This has led to many niche blogging sites on topics like health, cooking, gardening, diving, rock climbing, and flying. Niche sites also allow for guest bloggers to post articles on other bloggers' sites. Today, there are more than 100 million blogs in the blogosphere (the online community of blogs and bloggers) (Gunuelius, 2016).

Recent blog posts are very different from those that were made when blogs where new to the internet. Blog entries now contain multiple links, both to other blog entries by the same blogger(s) or to other sites. A wide variety of multimedia is also embedded into posts, from images and audio through to video. For this to occur, a number of sites have appeared that offer basic blogging templates (for example, WordPress) through to ones that rely exclusively on multimedia (for example, Glogster where each post is a multimedia-based poster). A number of other kinds of blogging also exist including vlogging (video blogging), and microblogging (for example, using Twitter or Tumblr). Perhaps the most famous site for blogging is Facebook.

Generally, though, all blogs hosted on their own website have a similar layout, contain an archive, a feed, and blogrolls, and require comment management. All blog posts are contained in a blog archive, and when an updated post is made, a really simple syndication (RSS) feed can be used to syndicate the entry and allow an aggregator to automatically collect the latest post for blog members to read. An RSS feed is a file that is used to subscribe to a place like a blog, podcast, or a website, and when those places are updated with new information, it is pushed to the aggregator. News aggregators are useful in that they utilize RSS to curate content automatically. This saves you checking all of your saved links for new information which may or may not be there, and allows you to see what is new – all in one place. A number of news aggregator applications and websites exist (for example, Feedly, Feed Wrangler, and Pulse). A blogroll contains all the links to other blogs or sites that are of interest to the blogger, or that are similar to the blog being read. A number of blog hosting sites offer a built-in link manager to generate this content.

Aside from these aspects, which are largely automated, managing comments is important for a blog. Comments can be the life of the blog, and offer direct involvement in a conversation with other commenters, or with the blog author(s) themselves. Comments also allow for features such as trackbacks (or pingbacks), which is a means of providing a link to a comment or article on another blog that your blog readers can then see and interact with. Monitoring systems are important as comment posts will also at some point receive spam, either from a person or a bot, and a visit from a troll.

Essentially, blogs are all about communication. A blog with a lot of content is generally going to reach a wider audience than one with only a few articles or links, or just static information. If content is regularly updated, this will ensure more comments and potentially more visitors. Visitors to the blog site will engage in some form of interaction with the blog when they visit, they will follow links to archived posts or other sites, watch videos, listen to audio, or leave a link or comment on an entry.

Wikis

A wiki is basically a dynamic web site where anyone can edit anything anytime they want using any web browser, and this operates on a principle of trust. Essentially a wiki is a server-side program that allows for collaboration in order to form the content of the site, allowing users to add, remove, or modify available content. They enable documents to be written collaboratively and quickly, hence the phrase 'wiki wiki' (meaning fast in Hawaiian) was coined (Leuf & Cunningham, 2002). This term was, in fact, originally used to refer to the first software to be called a wiki: Wiki Wiki Web, which was installed on the net in 1995, and this site is still visitable today.

A wiki can be thought of as a database that uses hypertext to keep track of entries and interlinked information to create a knowledge base. The term wiki can be used to refer to either a website, or to the software used to create the website. Any wiki allows users to change, edit, add, or reorganize content through a simplified browser-based web interface that has support for hyperlinks, the use of a simple syntax for the creation of new pages, and the formation of crosslinks between internal pages. It is not necessary to know any HTML (hypertext markup language). A user can review the history of changes, edits, and additions of the page that they are working on, or preview their changes before publishing them to the internet. Users can also use a sandbox for testing and experimenting with wiki syntax if they are just starting out. The simplest wiki program allows users to create and edit content, and more advanced wikis have management components that allow for a moderator to accept or reject any changes. Although wiki pages can be maliciously deleted, they can also be easily resurrected from a change history file. Those wiki pages that are bot maintained are also automatically regenerated if they are deleted.

There are also wiki farms where two or more wikis run on the same web server and share common components. They also offer a global search facility which can help when scanning through all the different individual wikis housed on such a site.

Perhaps the most well-known wiki web site is Wikipedia.

Essentially, the concept of 'open editing' that wikis provide has had a profound and subtle effect on wiki use, encouraging democratic use of the internet and promoting content composition by any user regardless of technological savvy (Leuf & Cunningham, 2002). This means that a wiki article becomes the sum of knowledge of all the people who have contributed to shaping it, and acts as a group created database. It is for this reason that a wiki can potentially become an excellent source of knowledge.

Ultimately, wikis are all about community, and today, a wiki on almost any topic can be found from travel (for example, Wikitravel, a worldwide travel guide) to city specific wikis (for example, Auckland.Wiki). Wikis cover a diverse range of subjects that support many communities (for example, artists, collectors, writers), and so they are a useful means of being able to expand community involvement and develop interest in specific subjects or activities. People worldwide can work collaboratively on online documents to create a range of peer produced content.

3

How can I use blogs and wikis in the classroom?

Blogs are proving to be an effective and valuable technology tool for learners and instructors. They can be used to extend the classroom from beyond the confines of the school setting, and they can be worked on at any time and from almost any internet connected device. This feature also applies to wikis. Blogs and wikis can motivate learners who might not necessarily participate in the classroom, provide media literacy opportunities, become spaces for collaboration and discussion, and enable scaffolded learning to occur. Further, the open-ended functions of wikis lead not only to collaboration, but to the reconceptualization of the functions of authorship and readership. Learners, as readers, must take on the role of arbitrator, editor, monitor, and writer, and exposing them to the construction and maintenance of a wiki can lead them to critically analyze the shared space within which they will now have to read, write, and think.

Teachers are using blogs in many ways in the classroom context which include setting blogs as writing assignments and as a method for both them and their learners to track progress of projects and class work. Blogs can promote analytical and critical thinking, while developing a community (Yang, 2009). Blogs can also combine the best of solitary reflection, with the social interaction afforded by interactive comments (Yang & Chang, 2011). Blogs can also promote associational, creative, and intuitive thinking, and are a powerful medium for increasing access and exposure to quality information.

On the other hand, wikis are being used in the classroom particularly for collaborative-based projects and providing students with a means to produce content rather than consume it (McLoughlin & Lee, 2007). However, it should be noted here that students prefer to create knowledge and produce their own content to that of editing other students' work (Lund & Smordal, 2006). Nonetheless, the power behind wiki use is the ease of editing and content generation from a digitally shared workspace. Wikis allow students to create web pages, link these pages together, and edit their own or each others' work very easily. Class wikis can be used as group collaboration projects, with the whole class monitoring content and making necessary edits and revisions. This editorial control in the hands of students gives them a sense of ownership and responsibility regarding the site. Wiki use can also help students develop collaborative skills, learn how to publish, negotiate with others, and agree on correctness, meaning and relevance.

No matter what the task, blog and wiki use can help foster both communication and community in the classroom. A number of means of putting blogs and wikis to use would include assigning students to work in pairs or in groups to write and post summaries of content covered during class as a review task. Students could also be given tasks that involve fact checking of blog posts and wiki entries compared to a source such as their textbook. This would, however, this would need to occur with prudence in countries that are using 'revised' textbooks in schools. A series of blog posts or wiki entries could also be assigned on certain topics, or each student could be provided with their own blog or wiki page to maintain and which concerns a specific interest or issue. The assigned blog or wiki could then be used as a scrapbook or portfolio of files that is used to document work completed on a unit, any project work, books and articles read, or even posts and entries regarding highlights of class time. Book and movie reviews, trailers, and summaries could also be worked on collaboratively and then posted to blogs and wikis, with other groups of students reacting in comments or on forums. Blogs and wikis also offer themselves support for a number of projects like oral history reports, and for detailing a series of steps or instructions, along with the hosting of student-created podcasts and screencasts. Storytelling development can also be fostered with either students working on writing in a round to write one paragraph or sentence with another student following, or working together collaboratively to produce the entire story. Blogs and wikis are able to detail the contribution level of each student to a project, their responses to peers, and edits that they have made, and to serve to archive not only their submissions on an assignment or task but their responses to it and the effort they have put into developing it. Blogs and wikis can then be used to showcase student work, and serve as an archive of submissions, before students post comments on other students' blogs and engage in the peer editing of others students' wiki content. Polls can also be used in conjunction with set blog and wiki tasks, topics, or assignments to survey students either for needs analysis purposes, or to determine student interest in the topic or their completion progress on an assignment.

Blogs and wikis are useful as organizers, and allow teachers to post learning objectives, assignments, and due dates, or even act as a place to post a weekly challenge such as riddle, with students posting potential solutions by the end of the week. Weekly summaries and reviews, teacher or student news, and classroom rules and codes of conduct could be hosted, along with notes and updates provided to students and other stakeholders on class events. PDF files of designated assignments, homework, worksheets, and handouts can be made available for download and archival purposes. Teachers can also provide links to students from a blog or wiki page that are much like those provided in WebQuests, and which are pre-screened and are able to provide specific and appropriate on-task information for students when using the internet or when working on a specifically assigned blog- or wiki-related task or activity. This is particularly important for young learners who can then begin to access internet-based content from a 'safe harbor' environment.

Every school district and educational institution has acceptable use policies in place regarding the use of the internet and computer networks, and these terms and conditions identify acceptable online access privileges and behavior. Policies regarding the display of any student work must be adhered to, and if specified, parental permission must be obtained before any student-generated content is published to a digitally shared collaborative workspace that is accessible by the general public. It is also important to ensure that each student is aware that there are limitations to the amount of personal and identifiable information that they should be publishing and sharing in a blog or wiki space.

Here are some of the pros and cons for blog and wiki use in the classroom.

- A fast and easy way to create a class website, but it takes time to update.
- Encourages participation that can then lead into classroom discussions, but it may prove difficult to keep students working on subjects that are relevant to class topics.
- An easy way to provide writing skills practice and improvement, but students may not write anything if they are not required to do so.
- Provides a place to collaborate on projects, but writing may be in a more casual style than that for formal submissions.
- A way to encourage shy students who don't talk in class to express themselves in other ways, but not necessarily quickly as it takes

longer to compose, edit, and post content, or respond to it using a blog or wiki medium.

- A means of granting authorship which gives students a feeling of ownership, but which could create competition between students.

- Easy for all students to read and see each other's writing, but it may be difficult for some students to follow as communication is asynchronous.

- It is a public form of communication which encourages writing for an audience, but students may only write a minimum if not required to do more with a set or directed task.

- They provide methods of sharing writing and ideas with people outside of the classroom, but this may mean a lack of confidentiality and privacy (although settings can be changed to adjust this).

- They can prove to provide an easy method for the instructor to digitally archive and collate student submissions and to assess levels of communication and collaboration, but they may meet resistance from those students who do not wish to use technology for learning.

4

What types of blogs and wikis exist?

There used to be a blog born every second (Keen, 2008), and now, this is every half-second, and today there is estimated to be 152,000,000 blogs on the internet (Gaille, 2013). Of course, not all of these blogs are active; some are abandoned, or lying dormant. Regardless, due to the sheer number of blogs that exist, there would be one for every subject area and topic imaginable, and they influence our decisions. They may help us decide on a product or which movie to see based on an individual review, or even change our lifestyle if we take action on suggestions made by a blogger presenting research on harmful or beneficial foods.

A number of blog types exist from so-called vanity projects that, despite being publicly accessible, are generally meant to be for an audience of friends and family, through to blogs that spread political messages, promote products, provide research data, give tutorials, and house podcasts and screencasts.

Essentially there are three types of blogs: the personal (writing by one person about themself and their day-to-day experiences), the corporate (providing updates about a company and personifying it), and specialist blogs (written by experts who provide insight into their specialization, or blog on it in terms of how it impacts or works in their lives). The specialist blogs in particular have come to see the internet turn into an easy-to-use database of information where specialists, like educationalists, put forward their thoughts and ideas, and build a discussion around them.

This is also reflective of wikis, which are built around a common community that shares their knowledge. The wiki then grows as people come together to edit it into an accurate knowledge base, and one that is reflective of the information and experiences that the authors, readers, and editors bring to it from their field of specialization. Unlike blogs, wikis are built with a sense of permanence (Godwin-Jones, 2003). Wikis that have been developed with this sense of permanence include those run by the Wikimedia Foundation (Wikipedia, Wiktionary, and Wikiquotes) through to cookbookwiki and fitnesswiki. Other categories for wikis, as Nations (2016) defines them, include entertainment, food and drink, game, health, political, product, and shopping, reference, religious, sports, and travel and geography.

"That's all very well," you may be saying, "but how do I locate the blogs and wikis that I'm looking for?" That's a good question. You can always begin with a Google search. You might also take a look at the 'List of wikis' on Wikipedia to find a wiki, and you can use the BlogSearchEngine or search RSS feeds using an aggregator when looking for blogs. They are out there, and they are easy to find.

5

What elements are behind effective blogs and wikis?

For blogs and wikis to be effective in the classroom, they need to be applied in ways that enhance student engagement in participative and collaborative learning. They also need to enhance students' multimodal literacy skills while providing them with a means of actively expressing themselves as they communicate on various topics and meet the six thinking levels of Bloom's revised digital taxonomy (creating, evaluating, analyzing, applying, understanding, and remembering) (Kent, 2015). For this to occur, it is important to regulate and structure student interaction with blogs and wikis so that content is produced edited and created according to desired learning objectives and, as James (2004) reminds us, giving control of the content to the learner. The role of the instructor then shifts, as Lamb (2004) states, to the setting up of problems that engage students as part of a learning community.

Establishing a classroom learning community is particularly valuable as it can change not only how students are taught but also how they experience the curriculum (Gablenick, MacGregor, Matthews & Smith, 1990), with shared knowledge, shared knowing, and shared responsibility at the heart (Tinto, 2003). This ties to Vygotskyian learning principles where knowledge is developed by interacting with other learners (especially the more knowledgable), through scaffolding, and through a zone of proximal development (ZPD) (Vygotsky, 1978). In this way, collective knowledge resides in the group rather than the individual (Nassaji & Cumming, 2000). Savery and Duffy highlight a number of instructional principles behind constructivist learning that can be applied to establish effective blog and wiki use with students, suggesting that teachers should:

- Provide reflective learning and practice by using authentic tasks;
- Include a number of taxonomies that encourage critical thinking, allowing students to provide their own solutions to problems;

- Create scenarios and set parameters that allow for problems to be solved;
- Provide a means for students to take ownership of the problem/learning; and
- Establish an environment where students are comfortable with making mistakes and are able to learn from making them.

Further, in terms of effective classroom assessment, blogs and wikis can be used for diagnostic, formative or summative assessment purposes. Diagnostic purposes may include asking students to post blog entries or create a wiki page concerning a topic before starting a new unit. Formative assessment may include providing ongoing feedback on a task or providing a summary of learning outcomes achieved from it. Summative assessment may involve blog and wiki use over the course of a semester or term, using it as an e-portfolio.

Ultimately, blogs and wikis encourage student interaction and collaboration in similar ways. Blogs and wikis also provide those learners reluctant, or unable, to speak up in a class an alternate avenue for their voice and a means to express themselves. Blogs encourage students to post articles, read and comment on other students' articles, and reflect on comments made on their own blog posts before considering if there is a need to post a response. Likewise, wikis encourage students to create articles to post, the reading and revising of other students' articles, and the need to reflect upon and review edits that other students have made to their own articles before deciding to keep those edits or not. The asynchronous nature of this kind of communication can prove advantageous here, as it provides learners with the time to think about what they are reading, and how they are going to respond.

6

How can blogs and wikis lend themselves to TESOL?

Finding the right one blogs and wikis to use in the classroom and in homework assignments, is important. They must not only be appropriate, but their use must also match with the topic and the assignment. Individual blogs and wikis on specific topics, over wikis that cover multiple topics in a general way (like Wikipedia), may prove more useful if using the sites as resources for assignments. Alternatively, a blog or a wiki could be started from scratch and either confined to the local network or posted on the internet, with learners developing all the content for it as part of any tasks set. In either case, and by their nature, blogs and wikis can provide an avenue for differentiation and the tailoring of instruction to meet student needs, and are perhaps viewed by many teachers of EFL and ESL as suitable for use in collaborative writing tasks. This is likely to be one of the most common ways that they are applied in the TESOL setting, but there are many other ways to use them in this context.

Any collaborative project is well suited to blog and wiki projects, providing a group activity where all students can be involved, and one where it is easy to see the evolution of student work and if they are working together equally (for example, by following individual blog posts and comments, or consulting the wiki article' change histories). As students write for a blog or wiki, they are consolidating their knowledge on a topic, and practicing and refining their reading and writing skills along with digital literacy and media literacy skills. As they write, edit, comment, and reply for a purpose, they are also creating ownership of the product that they are developing (Jatkowski Homuth & Piippo, 2012). While undertaking this process, peer-assessment and peer-editing also confirms for students that they are writing for an audience of at least their fellow students, and not just their teacher.

Campbell (2003) suggested that blogs be used as tutor, learner, or whole-class blogs, and in many ways, the uses that he sees for these can also be applied to wikis. Tutor blogs provide support for learning, links to various websites and resources including quizzes, and reminders about in-class tasks, all while encouraging learners to overcome their fears of reading in English and encouraging verbal exchange through comments. The learner blog could be run by individual students or by students working collaboratively in pairs or groups, predominantly in reading and writing classes where Campbell suggests that learners can post their thoughts on completed assignments and practice aspects of writing like journaling. The whole-class blog, which results from the collaborative effort of the entire class, can be applied with many different classes. In conversation classes it can be used as a bulletin board where learners can post messages, images, videos, and links related to classroom discussion, and it can be used to develop project-based language learning assignments that require research.

Horvath (2009), also sees blog use as a means of ensuring that the reading content for the course is student produced, with tasks set to take advantage of students developing and creating knowledge that they will need to complete future projects or tasks that are to be assigned later in the school term or semester.

In Saudi Arabia, Al Khateeb (2013) envisions the use of wikis in writing classes as aligning with tasks that arise from the use of the normal syllabuses, particularly when needing to develop the writing skills necessary for academic purposes. To this end, a blog or wiki could be applied to assist students in developing a process for writing, from a shared knowledge space, and using both cooperative means (working separately on pieces to create a whole) as well as collaborative means (working together to create the whole). However, Aydin and Yildiz (2014) found that wiki use with students in Turkey lead to various results depending on the collaborative task applied (argumentative, informative, or decision-making). The argumentative tasks prompted a higher rate of peer corrections, informative tasks yielded a higher rate of self-correction, and all tasks led students to focus more on meaning over form. Nevertheless, as a means of computer mediated communication, blogs and wikis can provide a variety of avenues for the use of task-based learning that incorporate authentic language and outcomes alongside support for student creativity. Mak and Coniam (2008) provide one such example from Hong Kong where incoming Year 7 high school students develop a wiki that illustrated the different facilities and features of the students' new school, which was then turned into a distributable brochure for their parents.

Blog post and wiki article topics can vary from review summaries of material and language points learned in class if the focus is largely on speaking and teaching conversation, or they can be used to write in a number of ways, such as essay style, if applied in the context of a writing class. Other blog and wiki uses may see students writing stories around a photograph, or using photographs as story starters. In this case, one student would post a photograph and the next would start to write the story, or a few sentences, before posting their own photograph for the next student again to continue the process. A wide variety of topics can suit such an activity, and it would lead to a diverse range of vocabulary and sentence structures being produced as all students complete the task. An alternative to this would be a student posting a short video of themself speaking a sentence or two of a story, or thoughts on a topic, followed by a video by the next student who would continue the story or topic with one or two sentences, and so on. These kinds of labeling techniques encourage listening and speaking as well as writing and reading, and they can be extended to a wide variety of topics such as things to do with friends and favorite things (Yamauchi, 2008), or even to tasks that require responses to sentences like 'You won't believe what I saw on the way to school!'.

Students can also use blog and wiki spaces as common areas for collating information required for group work or other in-class assignments. They may be able to collect links to songs, and YouTube and Vimeo videos that are reflective of language points such as the grammar being studied in class, and house these links on their blogs or wikis with example sentences or phrases. A blog series or a wiki article like this can also be set from class to class, or semester to semester, with different student groups adding to it over time to create a study guide. Jatkowski Homuth and Piippo (2012) also remind us that blogs and wikis can be used for journaling, providing feedback to students, giving opportunities for peer editing, and the showcasing content in, say, a portfolio. Blog and wiki collaboration can also occur amongst different classes located in different locations or countries, particular between languages other than English (LOTE) and EFL or ESL classes, and this can lead to the development of posts and articles such as a day in the life of students in another class. Blogs and wikis can also be used as travelogs of class excursions, or used to develop a travel brochure to different locations or even to different time periods, if this suits a text being read in class or any unit or topic discussion that may have arisen during class time.

Other ways that blogs and wikis can be used may include the development and posting of a book trailer to a blog post after a wiki has been developed around the reading of the book, with a different page for each main character and chapter of the text. Books and movie review posts and articles can also be created in-class and hosted on a blog or a wiki when teaching a unit on movies. In turn, when teaching a unit on food, blog posts and wiki articles might reflect students' favorite recipes. Students can also be assigned to post new words that they have learned each week to a blog post, or to generate a list in a wiki article. This would lead to the development of a collaborative dictionary, built from the new words that students have met throughout the term or semester. This vocabulary could be used with flash card applications (for example, Memrise), and provide content that teachers can in turn use for in-class review quizzes in conjunction with student response systems (for example, Plickers). Blogs and wikis can also provide an avenue where students can ask questions about language, topics discussed in class, and even assignment completion with peers or the instructor responding. In turn, this can lead to the development of a class frequently asked questions (FAQ) page.

Blogs and wikis can also be used in conjunction with other technology including talking avatars. Voki is one example of a customizable talking avatar that can be embedded into a blog or wiki page for free. Technology like this can add a more human feel to the blog or wiki, and promote the opportunity of a higher level of engagement with the learning material. For second-language learners it can also provide another avenue for using their own voices. Talking avatars can also prove particularly useful when relying on blogs and wikis for presentations, and for students to practice listening to their own pronunciation as well as their peers' and their teacher's. The variety of engaging materials and the many add-ons that can be embedded into a blog or wiki can lead to both language practice and assist with core task development, and they should be explored.

It is also advisable, when working with blogs and wikis, to use a rubric and to set a minimum number for posts and comments, replies to comments, as well as the minimum number of sentences and paragraphs that constitute an article. In this way students will know how hard they need to work to edit or create their end product, and the expectations that they need to strive to meet.

7

How can I start using blogs and wikis with students?

Today's students may be considered digital natives (Prensky, 2001) but do not assume that this means that they will be able to use a blog or a wiki from the get go. As with any other technological tool or task applied in the classroom, students will need to be made familiar with and its application. Clear expectations both for learning goals and the use of blogs and wikis need to be established, with this then followed through with a means of engaging students in the learning process to ensure that they work collaboratively to meet goals, and that what they create can be adequately assessed and then showcased. To achieve this, clear guidelines, similar to those that follow, are essential, and would need to be established.

Guidelines for using blogs and wikis with students

One – Keep clear expectations

Develop learning outcomes or goals initially, and then work with the technology to ensure the task being set aligns with those goals or outcomes. Then, determine how best to assess the blog and wiki use – diagnostic, formative, or summative. Further, provide clear guidelines for collaboration, posting and rewriting, as this will help students to maintain focus and stay on track, and it ensures that the mechanical aspects of any task can be met. It is vitally important to check school policy for social media use. Perhaps student photos are not allowed to be posted online at all, or they may require parents' permission or faces to be blurred. Students should be made aware that there are consequences for posting inappropriately, and written guidelines may be useful here.

Two – Develop over time

Keep a consistency with student blog and wiki work, and align this work with your expectations to ensure that students are reaching the goals set for achievement as they develop their blogs and wikis. If this is their first time, it may be better to start with a classroom blog or wiki that is developed slowly, with one assignment per week over a semester or term, or one that uses a single blog post or a single wiki page in one classroom session. If the choice for a classroom blog or wiki has been made, then it can also serve as a means of allowing archives of course worksheets and handouts, as well as a medium for updating students and other stakeholders (such as parents).

Three – Engage

Initially, engage students in the blog and wiki development process, either individually or as a class, by setting assignments that involve the use of a variety of blogs and wikis. Ideally, this can start out with students conducting assignments where they need to collect and then report on information gathered, and in turn store a synthesis of this information on a blog or wiki for presentation. Students could also be directed to collate materials for the development of multimedia blog and wiki posts, particularly by using sites such as Glogster. Reviewing other blog and wiki content can also inspire ideas to include on the classroom blog or wiki. As these tasks are introduced, it is important to demonstrate how to go about accomplishing them, so that students become familiar with the sites, and how to use them.

Four – Collaborate

The strengths arising from blog and wiki work are that they lend themselves easily to socio-constructivist models of teaching and learning, where learning is viewed as a process of peer interaction that is mediated and structured by the teacher (Jordan, Carlile & Stack, 2008). To this end, teachers can set specific tasks where students work as pairs or in groups to create their own blog posts or wiki pages on a topic in order to complete an assignment or to develop notes for a presentation. This would see students working around a teacher-directed theme to achieve specific learning goals while also being able to nominate who will take on certain roles and, when working on longer projects, if these roles will be swapped throughout a term. Students should also be reminded to preview anything that they work on before making a final blog post or wiki entry, and the teacher should ensure that they know how to revise their posts and edits if they wish to change these later. After the posts and edits have been made, encourage discussion of them while providing suggestions and on-going feedback.

Five – Assess

Any use of blogs or wikis for assessment must ensure that the tasks set for use with them aligns to the learning goals of the course, is reflective of course content, and is student-centered, with evaluation conducted by self, peer, or teacher. Consider also providing on-going feedback by commenting on student comments, their edits, and their posts as the course progresses. This will help students maintain a focus on their tasks, improve in areas where they may have been lacking, and see them brought back on track if necessary. Feedback and assessment for blogs and wikis, as for many other uses of technology in the classroom, needs to be ongoing rather than consist of a singular instance at the completion of a task (Al-Kilidar & Johnson, 2009). If making a blog or wiki from scratch, posting the assessment rubric to the site is worthwhile. Also, teachers, depending on the age range of students and the teaching context, may also consider having students help with the development of a rubric that is based on designated learning objectives.

Six - Showcase

At the end of the task, students work needs to be showcased. Casting a digital spotlight on student work is important because it reinforces the notion that the students are producers of knowledge and content and not just consumers of it. In this way too, blog and wiki work also begins to function as an e-portfolio, which comes to highlights student and class work as it is developed over a semester or term. Further, blogs and wikis can be used to showcase events, like field trips or classroom milestones, as well as student work and assignments. It is these blog posts and wiki pages that can then be spread across social media, like Facebook, with some stakeholders (either parents, or the students themselves) wanting to share these classroom achievements with others.

8

How do I evaluate blogs and wikis?

Perhaps the most appropriate means available to evaluate a blog or a wiki, particularly in the TESOL context, is to use a prefabricated rubric based upon a Likert-type rating scale. Any such rubric should be presented to students beforehand so that they can understand what will be assessed and expected from them.

Evaluation rubrics, particularly those using indicators across several categories, are essential when assessing the quality of student work on any complex multimedia-based project. Although it is useful for the busy teacher to apply pre-made rubrics, it is even better if teachers formulate ones of their own that reflect their teaching environment and the points that they wish to assess. One good source for this is Rubistar, where there are a number of pre-made evaluation options as well as information on how to create unique context sensitive evaluation instruments. The rubrics section of the resources list contains several other rubric creation tools that may prove worthwhile to look over.

An important point to consider when evaluating student-created blogs and wikis is that multi-literacy and penmanship in digital spaces is somewhat different to the pen and parchment process. The trick is being able to adequately assess aspects of student language use as they create their blog posts and wiki articles while also taking into account the comments and responses that they make on other students' blogs, and the processes that they engage in during wiki content creation and editing. In either case, it is important to take into account and evaluate both the avenue of communication and the content that results, and to this end, a sample rubric follows, and it can be applied equally when using either blogs or wikis. It has been crafted to work with both, as the 'group work' assessment item has been split into three levels of criteria ('overall', 'blog only', and 'wiki only') with each intended to be applied as appropriate.

The rating scale used in the following rubric goes from 1 to 5, with 1 being poor, 2 fair, 3 average, 4 good, and 5 excellent. 'Average' is used as a midpoint so that students can see how each particular skill relates to peers. This allows teachers to identify those skills that are weak in individual students, and those that may need improvement.

Assessment Item	Assessment Criteria	Score
Organization	Layout is appropriate (headings, keyword use, succinct titles, hook).	1 2 3 4 5
	Text flows, and has readability.	1 2 3 4 5
	Follows writing conventions: Structure (introduction, body, conclusion).	1 2 3 4 5
	Paragraph (topic sentence, support, concluding sentence).	1 2 3 4 5
Content	Meets learning objectives.	1 2 3 4 5
	Provides a significant contribution to the topic.	1 2 3 4 5
	Shows insight and understanding of the topic.	1 2 3 4 5
	Presents a balanced viewpoint.	1 2 3 4 5
	Free of errors, and plagiarism.	1 2 3 4 5
	Broad range of evidence, with claims sufficiently supported.	1 2 3 4 5
	Citations provided.	1 2 3 4 5
Technical	Links to internal and external websites provided.	1 2 3 4 5
	Links, and media relevant and connected to topic.	1 2 3 4 5
	No copyright infringement.	1 2 3 4 5
	Metadata is accurate, tags are appropriate, social media links and RSS feed are established.	1 2 3 4 5

Assessment Item		Assessment Criteria	Score
Language		Clear and concise, logical use of language, no confusing sections.	1 2 3 4 5
		Terminology used correctly, and explained.	1 2 3 4 5
		No misspellings or grammatical errors.	1 2 3 4 5
Group Work	*Overall*	Extensive edits and revisions made by all group members.	1 2 3 4 5
		Individuals contributed equally.	1 2 3 4 5
		Individuals fulfilled any additional assigned editing roles.	1 2 3 4 5
	Blog only	Each individual commented on at least one other groups post.	1 2 3 4 5
		Each individual replied to at least one comment on their groups post.	1 2 3 4 5
	Wiki only	Each individual made error changes to another groups article.	1 2 3 4 5
		Each individual added meaningful details to another groups article.	1 2 3 4 5
		Each individual provided additional evidence (media or links) to another groups article.	1 2 3 4 5

Ratings: 1 Poor 2 Fair 3 Average 4 Good 5 Excellent

9

What tools are available for blog and wiki creation?

There are many tools that are freely available and from which to select and begin blog and wiki creation. Once you have chosen a site or a tool, then setting up the blog or wiki is usually straightforward, especially if you have elected to use a free hosting service rather than self-host.

A number of free hosting sites allow you to customize your blog or wiki by editing the code of the templates on offer, or by allowing you to import templates that you may have obtained from elsewhere. Most sites and tools also allow you to import a range of media elements to further personalize your digital space.

Some of the most popular online utilities to support blog and wiki creation are:

Blogs

Blogger.com will host your blog for free, and aside from being simple to use, it allows some level of privacy which makes it suitable for use as a class blogging site. From one account, you can create as many blogs as you wish, and determine who is allowed to comment on the content.

Edublogs.org allows teachers to create and mange their own and their students' websites. There is room for customization of design and the ability to add various media to this private and secure platform.

Kidblog.org is an easy-to-use safe, and secure publishing platform designed for students in grades K-12. There are a number of excellent features including privacy, password protection, no need for student personal information to be collected, and no advertising. It is free for up to fifty students per class.

WordPress.org is one of the most popular blogging platforms in use today as it is open source, and is easily customizable. The downloadable software for self-hosting purposes is much more flexible than what is available on the blogging platform.

MicroBlogging

Twitter deserves a mention here as it is useful for microblogging (posting short frequent updates). It allows users to post and read short 140-character posts called tweets.

Tumblr is a blogging platform open to those over thirteen years of age, with most users using pen names. Users can post on their blog, follow others, and search posts. It is unique in that posts are divided into media types: text, photo, quote, link, chat, audio, and video.

Wikis

PBworks (formerly PBwiki) is a real-time collaborative editing system with several solutions including one for educators. It offers a single workspace where student accounts can be created without email addresses, and easy editing without the need for coding.

PmWiki is a wiki tool that gives user access control over individual pages, so they can be set for access by specific people, and to have different passwords for each page. The software also allows for navigation trails through individual sections, insertion of tables, and a printable layout.

Wikidot offers members the ability to create a wiki-based website with forums, and they can create a community, and publish and share documents and content.

Wikispaces is a free wiki hosting service that provides educators with a means to monitor student progress in real time, the ability to easily create projects and assign them to students, editing tools, the means to monitor student progress in real time, and a social newsfeed.

10

How do I establish the use of a blog or wiki in the classroom?

When looking to establish the use of blogs or wikis in the classroom, several factors need to be considered, and these are outlined in the following steps.

Step One – The approach

Whether blogging or using a wiki, the path taken will always needs to start with a plan. Decide what the blog or wiki will be about, what students will do in the digital space, and if media will play a central role in the completion of tasks. For example, will students take photographs and video, or record audio? Will they write posts or construct articles around these media artifacts, such as describing events, telling a story, developing a podcast or screencast, or providing a virtual tour? Set the focus and approach to encourage students to create content that they are willing to share and that other students would be willing to read and link to. You should then be able to justify any blog or wiki use in terms of how it assists in the language learning process, and be ready to provide this rationale to various stakeholders (including parents, administration, and the students themselves). Finally, ensure that your plan matches with any policies set in place by your school. With all of this done, the next step involves selecting a tool.

Step Two – The tool

The right blog or wiki tool to use depends on the teaching and learning context that you find yourself working in, and a number of appropriate tools for use in the educational context have already been discussed. Yet, no matter the tool chosen, restrictions need to be set. Choices need to be made as to who can see posts and edit them, who can post articles and edit them, who can post comments and reply to them, and who may revert a wiki site to an earlier version. Other matters that need considering are the parts of the blog or wiki that are important to protect or lock from changes as well as the sections that may need moderating for appropriateness, and who is to be responsible for carrying out this task (teacher or student). It also needs to be decided if the site will be locally or externally hosted, and who will be able to join the site and view it. Once these decisions have been made, arrange access to the site for students, and ensure that all of them are able to register successfully. This also means ensuring closure of the digital divide (Mossberger, Tolbert & Stansbury, 2003), and any students who cannot access the blog or wiki at home or from a smartphone will need to be provided with access at school or some other alternative. Further, be prepared to reevaluate the appropriateness of the tool as students use it.

Step Three – Setting tasks

Decide on the kinds of tasks that the blog and wiki will be used for, and how these sit within your curriculum (or the associated topic) and your students' levels, and consider any methods of assessment that may be required, be they diagnostic, formative, or summative. Be consistent with the use of the blog or wiki: once a week in-class or for homework over a term; or once a month used as part of a review task. Above all, moderate student work to ensure that they remain on track and are posting and editing appropriately. Setting guidelines and handouts to assist them in this process will prove useful. In addition to having standard member roles for any tasks, it may be beneficial to assign specific group members to certain roles, or get students to assign these extra roles themselves (for example, post/article editor, citation editor, chief editor). The photocopiable section of this book contains several handouts for these purposes. A further point of note here is that inaccurate content or writing during task development can be used as learning opportunities about things like plagiarism, copyright, or language learning points.

Step Four – Content editing

After setting up a blog or wiki, students will either need to make a new post or create an article that can be edited, and each blog or wiki tool will be slightly different to use. However, creating a new blog post is often similar to typing an email in a web-based email client (for example, that provided by Gmail). All posts can be previewed before being posted, and edited by the post author(s) once they have been posted.

Leaving or replying to a comment is as simple as typing into the comment box and clicking a button such as 'Publish'. Almost all wiki software contains a 'Sandbox' where students will be able to play with the development of the wiki. Most wikis can be edited after clicking on a link such as 'Edit page', from where you can then enter and edit text. Some wiki coding may be required, and although not the same, it is very similar to HTML. A change history is also kept alive in a wiki, and clicking on a link such as 'Page history' would allow you to see who has made previous edits to the wiki along with the changes made. The history list can be used to revert the page to any previous incarnation as necessary. Each wiki page also has a commenting section that students can use to plan out their wiki page as they work, and the teacher can use it to provide encouragement and feedback on the task. To ensure that students stay on task when posting, commenting, replying, editing, and creating content, it may be necessary to develop handouts or use existing ones; for example, the format expected for blog posts, or a checklist for how to engage in editing an article on a wiki. Several handouts like these are available under the photocopiable section of this book.

Step Five – Sharing and assessing

Generate traffic to the blog or wiki. Visitors can be other students, or stakeholders such as parents. Ensure that site feeds have been established so that you do not have to continually check pages, but can use an aggregator to see when students are updating blog posts or editing wiki articles. Many wikis can also be set to email changes as students make them (as a daily or weekly digest rather than singular edits). Also, encourage students to provide readers with a reason to want to bookmark or share the blog post or wiki article; it needs to be creative or informative, and have social media buttons easily accessible. It is also important for students to have access to the RSS feed as this also informs them when peers have made posts and article edits. It also helps them to become familiar with the establishment of a personal learning environment (PLE), something recognized as important for 21st century learners and workers (Kent, 2016). Once the blog posts or wiki articles have been assessed and are ready for showcasing, it would be prudent to close the blog or wiki to revisions so that no further changes to the content can be made.

Step Six – Keep in mind
Define goals
Ensure that you have a focus from the start, both for the individual tasks set and for the overall rationale of using blogs and wikis in the first place.

Be consistent
Set tasks to use the blog and wiki regularly, especially if it is being used over the course of a semester or term.

Seek help
Provide avenues for students to ask for help when they need it, either from peers or from the teacher. You as the teacher should look for help if you need assistance with implementation.

Share

Provide social media buttons so that the post or article is easy to share, and encourage posts and articles to be written in creative and informative ways to encourage a desire in readers to share them.

Readability

Use bullet points, sub-headings, and bold and italic text to create posts and articles that are easily readable and well formatted.

Evolve

Technology is constantly changing, but with a background in blogs and wikis from this book providing key elements and a core of understanding that you can work from, it should be easy to keep up to date with any changes and what this may mean for developing blog and wiki use with students in the future.

Checklist

Use existing or fabricated checklists with students when they work to create posts and articles, and for when it is time for students to respond to, edit, or assess peer blog posts and wiki articles.

11

How would I use a tool to work with a blog and a wiki?

There are a large number of easy to use websites that provide blog and wiki hosting to educators for free, along with a number of tutorials on how to best use the sites. Alternatively, open-source software can be downloaded and set up to run from a local server. No matter the choice, both blogs and wikis are designed to offer visitors a means of interaction with the content, while plugins, modules, and widgets are able to expand the base functionality of the sites.

When using freely available blog and wiki services from any hosting provider, it is important to make decisions concerning usernames and who can view and edit posted content. Although both blog and wiki platforms are designed to allow any user to be a consumer and producer of content, it is not always prudent to use these tools with students, especially very young learners, and this may warrant a need to operate a closed blog or wiki. If operating an open blog or wiki, you may want to encourage students to use pseudonyms, and also decide if outsiders are able to make comments, reply to comments, or edit. Constant moderating of blog and wiki comments, as well as edits, would then be essential, and in this way, students can be protected from outside users who might begin to act inappropriately or irresponsibly. Once aspects like these have all been taken into account, the blog or wiki process can be initiated in a way that provides a range of learning opportunities for students and a world of varied instructional possibilities for teachers.

Please keep in mind that, although tools and websites do at times change the features that they offer and the layout of the interface, and may even become defunct, the following guides on getting started have been written in a way that any such changes will not impact on understanding the essential mechanisms behind the creation of a blog or wiki.

11A. Working with a blog

Preparation

Before establishing a blog for use with students, it may be worthwhile to review several of those that are available across the internet so that you can get an idea of how other teachers are using their blogs with their classes. One of the most popular blogging portals is WordPress which is available in a multitude of languages. It could prove a good option to choose for a blogging platform as it can either be used online by selecting a plan from a number of options, or by downloading the open-source application for a local install.

Step One – Getting started

To begin working with Word Press for blogging, head to their website and click 'Register'. Each time after that, click on 'Log in', enter your username and password, then click 'Log in'. You will then be able to enter the URL for your first site, and you can create as many sites as you would like. The 'My sites' link will take you to your sites, and allow you to switch between the sites under your account. The 'Reader' tab allows you to follow the sites to which you have subscribed. Clicking 'Update your profile' will allow you to change your 'Public display name' to a pseudonym, and to enter information about yourself and the sites in which your profile will appear. 'Account settings' can be used to change your 'Username', 'Email address', 'Primary site', and the 'Web address shown publicly' when posting, and 'Language' settings. You can also 'Manage purchases', adjust 'Security', and set 'Notifications' concerning new comments and likes on blog posts, 'Get apps' to manage WordPress sites across all devices, and take some 'Next steps' to alter the 'Theme' and 'Plan', to 'Start your first post', or to 'Create a page' such as an about us or contact us page.

Step Two – Customization

With a free WordPress plan, there are some customization options but some are reserved for those with a paid plan. Customization options include changing the way the blog looks and feels by being able to set a logo and tag line as well as a title, choosing a color palette for a background, changing fonts and header images, and changing the locations of menus. You are also able to change the nature of how a blog post displays by choosing between a full post or displaying an excerpt for the blog and archive pages, displaying an author bio on single posts, and choosing to display the date, categories, and tags associated with the post. Widgets can also be customized, like those that can be placed on the sidebar. The options are large and they range from blog stats and archived posts through to a calendar and pages that are available on the site. It is also important to note that the blog front page can be made 'Static' or it can be set to shoe 'Your latest posts'.

Step Three – Sites and page options

Click on 'My sites', then choose which of your sites that you want to work with, and you will be taken to that site's administration page. Here you can see the blog 'Stats' which include posting activity and post summaries. The 'Plan' option displays your current plan and allows for an upgrade if desired, the publish section offers a means to add 'Blog posts' and 'Pages', the personalize section offers a means to customize 'Themes' and 'Menus', and the configure section provides a means for 'Sharing' on social media and add 'People' to the site as 'Followers' or as 'Email followers' and assign them various roles such as 'Administrator', 'Editor', 'Author', Contributor', and 'Subscriber'. This is useful for adding students to a particular site's team, and assigning them different roles. Plugins and domain names can be added from here, and settings can be changed in 'Site profile', 'Privacy' (public, hidden, or private), 'Footer credit', 'Related posts', 'Change site address', are other options that are offered. There is also 'Start over' and 'Delete site'. The final option in the configure setting is 'WP admin' and this will take you to the WordPress 'Dashboard'.

Step Four – The dashboard

The WordPress dashboard offers an easy way to control all the behind-the-scene details concerning the management of your site, and it contains several modules that include: 'At a glance' (a count of total posts, pages, and comments, spam caught, and storage space), 'Quick draft' (a mini-post editor that can be used to post content or create a draft), 'Activity' (all the recent activity with options to approve or unapprove, reply, edit, see the history, mark as spam, and trash items), 'Your stuff' (your recent activity), 'What's hot' (the top and latest posts and news across WordPress.com), and 'Stats' (a graph of blog traffic and links to popular areas of your blog). The display of these items can be toggled on or off, and the display order can be changed. Also available is a navigation menu that provides links to all of the WordPress administration screens for 'Posts', the 'Media' library, 'Pages', 'Comments', 'Feedback' options, 'Appearance' options, 'Users', 'Tools', and 'Settings'.

Step Five – Creating and editing a page

You can create pages by clicking 'Pages' then 'Add new' from the dashboard, or by clicking 'Add' next to pages on the administration page. The pages added to the blog would provide readers with information 'About the blog' or with a means to 'Contact' the author of the blog. Once you have clicked 'Add', you will be taken to a what-you-see-is-what-you-get (WYSIWIG) editor which allows you to work with text and embed various media into the post. You can then add a 'Title' for the page and start to edit the content as you would in a normal word processing program. As you edit, a draft will be saved, or you can click 'Save' if you need to come back to the content later. You can set a 'Featured image' for the page and 'Preview' the edits, set 'Page attributes', and show 'Sharing' and 'Like' buttons'. Other options include a 'SLUG' or a URL friendly post title, 'Write an excerpt', set a 'Location', 'Allow comments' and 'Allow pingbacks and trackbacks'. After you have completed the editing process and made selections for the page, you can then 'Preview' it and, if satisfied, 'Publish' it to the site. To edit these pages at a later date, click on 'Pages' on the administration page. You will then be able to 'View' and 'Edit' each page, or send a page to the 'Trash'.

Step Six - Creating and editing a blog post

You can create blog posts by clicking 'Posts' then 'Add new' from the dashboard, or by clicking 'Add' from the administration page. Once you have clicked 'Add', you will be taken to a what-you-see-is-what-you-get (WYSIWIG) editor. which will allow you to proceed as in Step Five. You can set 'Categories and tags' for your post, a 'Featured image', 'Show sharing buttons' and 'Show like a button'. The post format can also be adjusted from 'Standard' to 'Aside', 'Image', 'Video', 'Quote', or 'Link'. Other options include those in Step Five, after which you can 'Preview' and 'Publish'. As a blog post it will appear on your site's main page in reverse chronological order. To edit the post at a later date, click on 'Blog posts' on the administration page. You will then be presented with an excerpt of each post and the date they were published, and you can 'Edit', 'View', peruse the 'Stats' of any post, or send it to the 'Trash'. When you are happy with the post, you can go to the front page of your site to see how it looks, and if it still needs some work, you can click 'Edit' at the bottom of the post to update it. You can also add a comment at the bottom of the post, as we can see in the next step.

Step Seven – Creating and editing comments and replies

To leave a comment on a post, navigate to the post that you want to leave a comment on, and click 'Leave a comment'. You will then be able to type your comments in a text box, and have the option to be notified of 'New comments via email', as well as being able to change the profile being used to make the comment. Once you are happy with your comment, click 'Post comment'. The comment will then be posted, and you will have the option to 'Edit' it, 'Like' it, or even 'Reply' to it. Various media, including images and links, can be added to comments and replies as appropriate.

11B. Working with a wiki

Preparation

Before getting started in creating a wiki, it might be prudent to review several other classroom wiki projects to see what other teachers are doing and what might be possible for your classes. PBworks, like other wikis, has a community of searchable wiki pages created by educationalists with wikis that provide professional development, facilitate teacher to teacher communication, or focus on content area teaching to various grade levels. A search through the directory and a browse through some of these sites, would be worthwhile.

Step One – Getting started

To begin working with PBWorks to create a wiki for student use, head to their website, then click on 'Get started', select 'EduHub', and choose the 'Free option'. The free service provides a single workspace for up to 100 users, classroom accounts, 2GB of storage, and a number of customizable options. At this point you will need to choose a name and URL for your wiki, and verify your account by email. Next, select the view settings for the wiki; 'Anyone' or 'Only people I invite'. Then move to your wiki workspace.

Step Two – Getting students on board

After setting up the wiki, you can add classroom accounts for students by clicking on 'Invite more people', then 'Create accounts for your students'. You can then choose the number of students and the permission level that they will have (editor, writer, reader). Names can then be added, with the wiki providing a username and password automatically, and all this can be printed as a list for distribution. All users can be found under the 'Users' tab where they can be viewed, deleted, have their passwords reset, and permissions changed.

Step Three – Workspace security

After students have been assigned their classroom accounts, it would be wise to set the workspace settings under 'Access controls'. Here you can chose who will be able to view the site, 'Disable commenting for readers', 'Let workspace users see the

User tab', or 'Let people request access to view and edit the workspace'.

Step Four – Monitoring changes via really simple syndication

Depending on the project, students may make up to fifty changes to a single wiki page in a classroom session, and it is difficult for one teacher to keep track of these changes, especially if there are thirty or more students in a class. A simple way to do this is to enable a really simple syndication (RSS) feed for the wiki site. This can be done under 'Access controls' by clicking on 'Notifications & RSS', and by default the site will 'Allow users to access this workspace's RSS feed and 'Enable email notifications for this workspace'. The RSS feed can be used by any news aggregator, and will provide an easy method to skim all the changes that students have been making. A number of news aggregator options are detailed in the resources list.

Step Five – Customizing

At this point you will want to rename the site 'Title' under 'Basic settings' and provide a description, then set the 'Space's time' and 'Contact email'. Other options here include changing 'Colors', importing a 'Logo' (for premium users), and 'Export' of pages.

Step Six – The front page

The wiki front page is the first page a visitor will see when arriving at the site, so it may be useful to edit this content to reflect news, announcements, and anything else of interest to students and visitors. The front page, like all the other wiki pages, can be edited by clicking on the 'Edit' tab, which will bring up a what-you-see-is-what-you-get (WYSIWIG) editor where you can enter content. You can also insert links to other pages or rename the page from here. A box is also provided so that you can describe the changes that you have made and saved (by clicking the 'Save' button). Links to other wiki pages, web addresses, and files can be added by clicking on 'Insert a link to a new page'. There are options to 'Upload files', and 'Insert image from URL', and the editor provides various means of inserting media including 'Video', and using 'Plugins' such as those including 'Interactive Media' to add a 'Voki'.

Step Seven – Creating pages

After setting up the wiki welcome page, it is time to add content and pages to the site by clicking on the 'Create a page' link from which you can 'Name your page' and put it in a folder if necessary.

Step Eight – Pages and files

The 'Pages & Files' tab allows you to access specific pages which also appear in a navigation sidebar on the first page of the wiki. After naming the page, you will be taken to a WYSIWIG editor and you can start adding content. After saving the content, you can view the page and send a link to others to let them know about the changes and to get feedback. As with all pages on the wiki, you can use the sidebar menu to 'Share this page', Put this page in a folder', 'Add tags', 'Control access to this page', 'Copy this page', and 'Check for plagiarism'. The Navigator 'Options' button will allow you to delete or move pages as well as 'Add folders' and 'Upload files' as needed.

Step Nine – Commenting

After you have made edits and have clicked on the 'View' tab to see the page, you will also be able to make comments on the page in the 'Add a comment' box. They can be seen only by site users. But the settings can be changed to make them visible to all who visit the site. Teachers can add comments that provide feedback, remind students of deadlines, and provide encouragement. Students can also use the comment box to provide encouragement and feedback to each other, sharing resources, and communicating asynchronously on aspects of the topic and any edits that might still need to be made. If the settings are enabled, comments can be removed by clicking 'Delete', and a 'Reply' can be left.

Step Ten – Reverting pages

If a page happens to be deleted in error, or someone has maliciously changed the content, you can always revert the page to an earlier incarnation. To do so, click 'Page history', and this will take you to a page history log that lists all saves of the page in reverse chronological order. You can delete these revisions, 'Compare' them, or select a revision to revert back to.

12

What are the key points behind blog and wiki use in the TESOL context?

A number of key points emerge when thinking of using blogs and wikis about teaching English to speakers of other languages, and some of the most important include:

- Blogs and wikis are a form of asynchronous computer mediated communication (CMC) that revolves around information sharing.

- Blogs are predominantly about communication, and wikis are about community, but both allow for collaboration.

- Both blogs and wikis allow students to produce content rather than consume it, and to react to existing content and influence it.

- A number of different types of blogs and wikis exist today, and all are reflective of the information and experiences that the authors and editors bring to them from their field of specialization.

- By their nature, blogs and wikis can provide an avenue for differentiation and the tailoring of instruction to meet student needs

- Blogs and wikis can provide a variety of avenues for the use of task-based learning that incorporate authentic language use, learning outcomes, support for student creativity, and the development of personal learning environments.

- The strengths arising from blog and wiki work are that they lend themselves easily to socio-constructivist models of teaching and learning, where learning is viewed as a process of peer interaction that is mediated and structured by the teacher.

- It is important to regulate and structure student interaction with blogs and wikis so that content is produced, edited, and created according to desired learning objectives, and gives control of the content to the learner. The role of the instructor then shifts to be that of establishing contexts and setting up problems that engage students as part of a learning community.

- The editorial control offered by both blogs and wikis in the authorship process gives students a sense of ownership and responsibility to these sites and their content.

- Students prefer to create knowledge and produce their own content to that of editing others' work, but peer editing and assessment is still crucial. For example, critical thinking skills can be promoted while students learn how to evaluate their own drafts, and while they provide feedback to peers.

- Clear expectations both for learning goals and the use of blogs and wikis need to be established, and then followed through with a means of engaging students in the learning process, ensuring that they work collaboratively to meet goals, and that what they create can be adequately assessed and then showcased.

- The asynchronous nature of this kind of communication can prove advantageous, as it provides learners with the time to think about what they are reading and how they are going to respond, with the shared responsibility of task development reducing cognitive load while providing social support.

- In terms of effective classroom assessment, blogs and wikis can be used for diagnostic, formative, and summative assessment purposes. Diagnostic purposes can include asking students to post blog entries or create a wiki page concerning a topic before starting a new unit. Formative assessment can include providing ongoing feedback on a task or providing a summary of learning outcomes achieved from it. Summative assessment can involve blog and wiki use over the course of a semester or term, using it as an e-portfolio.

- It is important to evaluate and take into account both the avenue of communication and the content that results.

- Set a minimum numbers for posts, comments, replies to comments, and sentences and paragraphs that constitute an article, along with any rubric used in assessment. In this way, students will know how hard they need to work on editing or creating their end product, and the expectations that they need to meet.

- Once the blog posts or wiki articles have been assessed, close the blog or wiki to revisions so that no further changes to the content can be made.
- Be able to justify any blog or wiki use in terms of how it assists in the language learning process, and be ready to provide this rationale to various stakeholders (including parents, administration, and the students themselves).

13

Lesson plan guides, and example implementation

Provided here are lesson plan guides, as well as an example for implementing blogs and wikis in the educational context. The guides are meant to assist in the understanding of how to develop a detailed lesson plan and to help describe what each component and stage of a lesson may cover. The example implementations are intended to provide a use-case scenario detailing the techniques required to apply the use of blogs and wikis in real world settings.

The content covered here includes:
- Lesson plan general guide
- Lesson plan guide for blogs
- Example implementation: Blogs
- Lesson plan guide for wikis
- Example implementation: Wikis

Lesson Plan General Guide	
Teaching Context	
Level of Proficiency and Maturity	Student language level (e.g. beginner, intermediate, advanced). Student age range (e.g. young learners, adults).
Lesson Length	Time allotted for the class (e.g. 35-45 minutes).
Lesson Topic	Major theme or focus of the lesson (e.g. numbers and time).
Objectives	Lesson aims (e.g. to teach students how to tell the time and date accurately).
Outcomes	Learning outcomes (e.g. students will be able to read analog and digital timepieces).
Relevant Prior Learning	Anything that students need to know before starting work on this lesson's content (e.g. students need to have completed Chapter Two of the book, and have previously met language associated with appointments, calendars, and timekeeping).

Teacher Preparation	
Hardware	Types of computer or peripherals required (e.g. USB sticks, MP3 players).
Software	Name of software used (e.g. Photo Story 3, Microsoft Word).
Webpage Links	Hyperlink to web resources (e.g. www.google.com).
Additional Resources	Other necessary materials for the lesson (e.g. handouts, worksheets, textbooks).

Procedure			
Stage and Timing	**Objective**	**Teacher**	**Students**
Review Stage (if required, 5 minutes)	Focus of stage (e.g. encourage the use of previously acquired language).	Indicate what the teacher says and does in each stage of the lesson.	Provide expected examples of student behavior.

Warm-up Stage/Pre-Technology Use (10 minutes)	Focus of stage (e.g. introduce new concepts and language to students in a meaningful manner).	Indicate what the teacher says and does in each stage of the lesson.	Provide expected examples of student behavior.
Main Stage/ Technology-based Activity (20 minutes)	Focus of stage (e.g. allow students to utilize technology to become familiar with and apply the concepts and language content introduced in the lesson).	Indicate what the teacher says and does in each stage of the lesson.	Provide expected examples of student behavior.

Practice Stage (15 minutes)	Focus of stage (e.g. allow learners to utilize the skills and language that they are expected to acquire during the lesson in a practical way).	Indicate what the teacher says and does in each stage of the lesson.	Provide expected examples of student behavior.
Lesson Summation Stage/Post-Technology Activities (10 minutes)	Focus of stage (e.g. instructor reinforces the importance of language concepts and skills acquired, stating how they will be useful in forthcoming lessons).	Indicate what the teacher says and does in each stage of the lesson.	Provide expected examples of student behavior.

Further Considerations	
Follow-Up Activities	Prepare material that can be applied in a follow up class. Also, be ready with activities for students who complete their class work earlier than expected.
Contingency Plan(s)	Always prepare an alternate teaching scenario in case of any problems. For example, a sudden power outage, or a timetabling issue could make the assigned room unavailable.
Evaluation	Reflect on what worked well, and what did not, and how you might deliver the lesson differently or improve upon it when running it again.

Lesson Plan Guide for Blogs	
Teaching Context	
Level of Proficiency and Maturity	Beginner to advanced. Adaptable for use with young learners through to adults.
Lesson Length	Suitable for a couple of lessons over a week. Homework completion components. Time allotted for each class: 50 minutes.
Lesson Topic	Food, cooking.
Objectives	1. Enhance communication skills through collaborative learning, presentations, and writing and speaking development. 2. Strengthen multiple literacies (computer literacy, digital literacy, and English literacy).
Outcomes	1. Students identify significant points on a topic, and use these in to develop blog posts and presentations. 2. Transfer current knowledge into learning, using and understanding technological systems.
Relevant Prior Learning	None required. Blogging and wiki experiences helpful.

Teacher Preparation	
Hardware	Computers or tablets with internet access for each group of students. USB sticks or Google Drive for storage.
Software	WordPress applications, or access to the website. Access to various media for development support (e.g. Google Images, and YouTube).
Webpage Links	WordPress.com www.epicurious.com www.taste.com.au Other food and cooking websites as appropriate to student level and age group.

Additional Resources	Handouts*:
	    • Pre-blog teacher considerations
	    • Pre-blog student considerations
	    • How to write a blog post
	    • Peer checklist – blog post

*Available under 'Photocopiable content'.

Procedure – Day 1 of 3			
Stage and Timing	**Objective**	**Teacher**	**Students**
Introductory Stage (5 minutes)	The topic of food and cooking is introduced. Traditional dishes for the host country can be provided to students.	Introduce the traditional foods of their country, and their favorite traditional dishes.	Students begin to think about their country and the traditional dishes that are their favorites.
Warm-up Stage/Pre-Technology Use (20 minutes)	Students work in small groups, to discuss each other's traditional foods and favorite traditional dishes.	Assist students as required. Provide question prompts: What are your country's traditional foods? What is your favorite traditional food? How is it prepared?	Students work together to discusses each other's traditional foods, their favorite traditional dishes, and how these are prepared.

Main Stage (15 minutes)	Students present their traditional foods to the class, and their favorite food.	The presentation can be used as an assessment if desired.	Students should each provide a short one-minute presentation.
Lesson Summation Stage/Post-Technology Activities (5 minutes)	Homework is set for students to either video themselves preparing the food, or finding a video of someone else preparing their food. The audio must be in English, or the student can provide an English voice-over.	Provide links to various cooking websites that may prove useful (e.g. Epicurious, Taste).	Students will prepare a video of themselves preparing their favorite traditional food, or a link to someone else preparing it.

Procedure – Day 2 of 3			
Stage and Timing	Objective	Teacher	Students
Review Stage **(5 minutes)**	Go over the class content from the previous lesson, and provide a short introduction on how to edit with a blog.	Confirm that the students have created a video, or have found a link to one suitable to use with blogging.	Students should have prepared a video, or have a link to one that is suitable.
Warm-up Stage/Pre-Technology Use **(5 minutes)**	Provide student access to the teacher-prepared blog page, and tips on editing with it (e.g. how to add a link, add an image, upload a file or embed a video).	Ensure that all students can access the blog, and are able to work with the editor. Review the 'Pre-blog teacher' handout*.	Students should be able to log onto the blog site, and begin working with the post editor. Have students review the 'Pre-blog student' handout*.

*Available under 'Photocopiable content'.

Main Stage (35 minutes)	Students work in groups of three to assist each other in creating a recipe page on the blog for their dishes.	Provide student groups with a layout to follow (e.g. picture of dish, recipe: ingredients and procedure, then a video of food preparation and cooking.	Students work in groups to assist each other in developing their posts, working with the 'How to write a blog post' handout*, as well as the guidelines for the post-format.
Lesson Summation Stage/Post-Technology Activities (5 minutes)	Students should have their post at a ready-to-publish stage, and need to review it a final time.	Ensure that all students have completed their blog page successfully. Provide the 'Peer checklist – Blog post' handout* for homework.	All components of the blog post should be complete, and the post published. Students will review another blog for homework using the handout provided.

*Available under 'Photocopiable content',

Procedure – Day 3 of 3			
Stage and Timing	**Objective**	**Teacher**	**Students**
Review Stage (5 minutes)	Students are reminded of their homework, and that they should submit their completed checklists to their peers.	Ensure that all of the peer checklists are distributed to students for review.	Students review the checklist, and if necessary ask questions to their peers about it.
Warm-up Stage/Pre-Technology Use (15 minutes)	Blog post review.	Ensure that students have access to their blog, and are able to edit their posts if they wish.	Students edit their post while taking into consideration the feedback provided by their peers.

Main Stage (20 minutes)	Individual presentations answering: What is the dish? Why is it a favorite? How is it made? What does it taste like?	Students will give a short presentation of their blog post (perhaps one to two minutes each)*.	Students provide a presentation regarding their dish, and how to prepare it.
Lesson Summation Stage/Post-Technology Activities (5 minutes)	Share the blog content with various stakeholders as appropriate. Lock the blog posts from any further edits, comments, and replies.	Assist students in sharing their blog post with peers or parents.	Students can archive their post in an offline portfolio, or share it with others.

*An extra day will be required for presentations if the class is a large one.

Further Considerations	
Follow-Up Activities	If the teaching context allows, students can demonstrate in the classroom. Excursion to a local market. Activities relating to festivals and culture.
Contingency Plan(s)	The next lesson in the course syllabus should be ready in case there is a problem at any stage of blog development. Alternatively, some language games can be prepared to fill in the time if technological problems occur. Several activity sheets for review of previous material should be prepared to allow those students who complete their scripts or recording to keep busy with language content.
Evaluation	What are the biggest frustrations for implementation? Can these be remedied next time? What are the successes of the lesson? What did students get out of this activity? Can more language practice be provided?

Example Implementation:
Blogs

The Teaching and Learning Context

A wide range of possibilities exist for the use of blogs with second-language learners. A blog can be used for a single class period to develop, revise, and then post a paragraph or an entire article, and blogs can be applied over a semester or term when working on more extensive projects or a series of pieces for a portfolio. For the latter case, the example of implementation presented in this section of the book presents a ten week outline for the development of a variety of language skills over the course of a term. It is suitable for developing blog use with students who are studying in a general English communication program within a college or university setting. The tasks and activities can be adapted to suit a variety of approaches that include communicative language teaching (CLT), task-based language learning (TBL), competency based language learning (CBLL), or project-based language learning (PBLL). The project selected here is that of developing an online newspaper called The Global Times.

Teaching Material

When using blogs in the classroom, the teaching material can be broken down into three parts: the software, the hardware, and the activities or tasks selected as appropriate for the learning context.

The software

Depending on your teaching context, the choice of blog software varies. It generally comes down to a matter of how accessible the content can be. For example closed for use with very young learners providing them with a safe-harbor environment from which to work; open at a global level for anyone to view and comment on when used with adults. The resources list presents several choices and there should be at least one that potentially offers the best options for your intended use and with which you feel comfortable when using with your students. It is likely that this choice will also come down to the ages of your students as well as the teaching locale (for example, grade school, university, or private institute).

The hardware

Depending on how and where the blog is to be accessed by students, a number of different technological requirements regarding hardware will need to be met. If you are working in a bring-your-own-device (BYOD) environment, you will need to make sure that the students bring their devices as required, and that they have the associated applications installed. If students are using the computers available at school, then the computer lab or computer room may need to be booked. If you are setting blog use for homework, then you will need to ensure that students are all students are able to access the hardware required to complete any set blog work and to use the internet. An alternate is to have students work on blog posts during class time in a traditional manner, using pen and paper, and then digitizing this for homework.

Learning content

A wide variety of tasks and activities are suited to blog use, with the tasks and activities chosen depending on the age and maturity levels of learners, their language level, the teaching environment (grade school, university, private institute), and the desired learning outcomes.

Procedure

For blog use to be successful, it is important to keep posts updated. It is also important to set clear expectations for learning goals with a means to engage students in the learning process as they work on their blogs, and to ensure that they are working collaboratively to meet these goals. What they are in turn developing can be adequately assessed for improvement in their learning and language abilities, and is able to be showcased. For this to occur, blog use will require active participation on the part of students, and this participation can be conducted in an asynchronous manner, providing them with time to compose comments or replies, as well edit blog posts. The editorial control on offer through the medium can also grant students a sense of ownership and responsibility to the site and the contents that they develop. To this end, and to maintain interest in blog projects, it may also be prudent to incorporate aspects of students' posts, comments, and replies within classroom discussions. Yet, no matter how blogs are used in the classroom, it is important to evaluate and take into account aspects of how students are using the avenue for communication, and producing the content that results.

Week one – Blog familiarization

When starting out using a blog, it is advisable to provide an introduction to the software that has been chosen, and familiarize students with the mechanics of how to post and edit blog articles, comment, moderate comments, and reply. This can be achieved by using a screencast, along with an associated worksheet, so that students are able to engage in language practice while becoming familiar with the blog process and what will be required of them throughout the remainder of the course. An overview of the tasks and objectives intended to be achieved by the end of blog use will also be important to introduce to students here, so that they can understand why they need to be familiar with blog use, how it all ties in to their learning goals, and how it can benefit their language skills.

Week two – Newspaper project

Students are informed of the topics, how the online newspaper project will be conducted, and that each group will ultimately be responsible for developing content for one of six sections of The Global Times newspaper. These sections can align strictly with textbook topics, or they could be developed to align with student interests, hobbies, or associations of which they are members. Each group of students can work on the same section each week, with the best aspects of each group's content making the final contribution to an official newspaper article on that topic.

Week three – Advice columns

This week can see students prepare questions that they would like to have advice on, with another group then researching and preparing answers. Alternatively, the teacher can provide the questions with appropriate links to obtain the answers. This kind of activity would be able to dovetail with a number of units, including those on injuries and seeing a doctor through to those providing guidance on study skills.

Week four – Reviews one

For this week, students could develop a digital story, with associated images and video components to review a book, movie, or an event like a concert. This could be completed in conjunction with a unit on entertainment, or hobbies.

Week five – Reviews two

Following on from the previous review, students could review a meal at a local restaurant using a rating scale that they have developed. Students would be able to review any restaurant on or near their campus, with appropriate images, and this can be completed in conjunction with a unit on food or cooking.

Week six – Recipe

Students can develop a written recipe based on their favorite food. The recipe would need to detail the ingredients, preparation, and method accurately, and include a photo of the prepared dish as well as an accompanying step-by-step video. This can tie to a unit on food or cooking.

Week seven – Tours

Students can develop a virtual tour using their smartphone to make video and audio recordings and to take photos. They could develop a walking tour of the campus. Alternatively, they could create a neighborhood tour, highlighting the best places to do certain activities in that area of town. This could dovetail with a unit on family and home life, school, or directions.

Week eight – Interviews

An example task for this week could see students conducting interviews on campus with native English speaking teachers. They would need to be able to develop appropriate interview questions on their topic, as well as have the necessary hardware to video or audio record their interview. The interview media could then be posted to the blog with an associated written summary underneath.

Week nine – Finalization

In this week of blog use, students would need to polish their articles by conducting last minute edits, taking peer comments into consideration, and selecting the final best pieces from all groups' articles to complete their section of the newspaper.

Week ten – Launch party

In this week of the class, students would be able to present one section of the blog as part of an 'official' newspaper launch. This can be completed as a class activity with another class, or with other stakeholders invited to attend.

Lesson Plan Guide for Wikis	
Teaching Context	
Level of Proficiency and Maturity	Beginner to advanced. Adaptable for use with young learners through to adults.
Lesson Length	Suitable for several lessons over a week. Homework completion components. Time allotted for each class: 50 minutes.
Lesson Topic	Travel
Objectives	1. Enhance communication skills through collaborative learning, presentations, and writing and speaking development. 2. Strengthen multiple literacies (computer literacy, digital literacy, and English literacy).
Outcomes	1. Students identify significant points on a topic, and use these in a presentation based on wiki articles that they have developed. 2. Transfer current knowledge into learning, using and understanding technological systems.
Relevant Prior Learning	None required. Blogging and wiki experiences helpful.

Teacher Preparation	
Hardware	Computers or tablets with internet access for each group of students working together. USB sticks or Google Drive for storage.
Software	Online wiki software (e.g. PBWorks). Access to various media for development support (e.g. Google Images, and YouTube).
Webpage Links	PBworks.com www.lonelyplanet.com www.tripadvisor.com (other travel sites appropriate to student language level and age group)
Additional Resources	Handouts*: • Pre-wiki teacher considerations • Pre-wiki student considerations • How to write a wiki article • Peer checklist – wiki article

*Available under 'Photocopiable content'.

Procedure – Day 1 of 3			
Stage and Timing	**Objective**	**Teacher**	**Students**
Introductory Stage (15 minutes)	Students bring a souvenir item from a trip to class, and use it to introduce the topic of travel.	Students need to be reminded to bring their item at least a week before, as well as the day prior.	Students will talk about their item in front of the class for at least one minute.
Warm-up Stage/Pre-Technology Use (5 minutes)	Students work in groups to create a travel wiki on a specific country, with page topics on: a short history of the nation, 'must see' sites, best times to travel, daily budget, and foods to eat.	Divide the class into groups, and provide them with suggestions to start creating their wiki articles and pages on a specific country.	Students form groups, and decide on the country that they will be creating wiki articles about, and who will be the main person responsible for each topic.

Main Stage (20 minutes)	Brainstorming and resource collection. Using websites and collecting various media. The final product should contain at least 50 words a topic for beginners, 100 words for intermediate students, and 200 words for advanced students.	Teacher assists students in brainstorming ideas on each topic, and for each article that the students will write. Teachers can take this opportunity to go through the 'pre-wiki teacher considerations' handout*.	Students begin to form points for their article and collect associated images (e.g. pictures and video).
Lesson Summation Stage/Post-Technology Activities (10 minutes)	Students are assigned additional wiki roles, and are provided with the 'pre-wiki student considerations' handout*.	Introduce students to the additional roles that they need to play when working on their wiki.	Students select who becomes the article editor, the citation editor, and the chief editor.

*Available under 'Photocopiable content'.

Procedure – Day 2 of 3			
Stage and Timing	Objective	Teacher	Students
Review Stage (10 minutes)	Go over the class content from the previous lesson, and provide a short introduction on how to edit with a wiki.	Confirm that students have prepared notes and various media that relates to their assigned topic, and are ready to create their wiki page.	Students should have prepared notes and media ready to create a wiki article on their topic.
Warm-up Stage/Pre-Technology Use (5 minutes)	Students post their articles under the main travel section page of the teacher-developed wiki.	The teacher helps students to post their pages to the designated areas of the wiki.	Students prepare to edit their wiki article, and enrich it with media.

Main Stage (30 minutes)	Students complete their wiki article on the topics they have chosen using the handout provided.	Help students work through the handout to develop their wiki article.	Students work through the 'how to write a wiki-article' handout* to develop their wiki page.
Lesson Summation Stage/Post-Technology Activities (5 minutes)	Provide students with the 'peer checklist – wiki article' handout*, so that they can complete it for their fellow members' articles. Inform students that they will need to present the information about their country in the next class session.	Ensure that students will be able to complete their articles for homework, if not already complete, and that they need to take into consideration the suggestions from the 'peer checklist – wiki article'*.	Students will complete, and then pass the 'peer checklist – wiki article'* to peers. All students will complete their article by the end of class, or they will need to do so for homework.

*Available under 'photocopiable content'.

Procedure – Day 3 of 3			
Stage and Timing	Objective	Teacher	Students
Review Stage (5 minutes)	Go over the previous class content, and remind students that their wiki articles and in-class presentations are due.	Confirm that students have completed their wiki articles, and are ready to practice their presentation.	Wiki articles should be fully developed, with the students ready to present them.
Warm-up Stage/Pre-Technology Use (10 minutes)	Provide time for students to practice going through their presentation.	Ensure that all students are ready to present and provide guidance for those students who still require it.	Students practice delivering their presentations together.

Main Stage (30 minutes)	Presentations delivered, and assessment completed.	Assess student presentations and wiki work using prefabricated rubrics, such as those provided in the evaluation section.	Students present their wiki travel articles to the class for assessment.
Lesson Summation Stage/Post-Technology Activities (5 minutes)	Archive wiki content, and share the material with various stakeholders as appropriate. Lock the wiki pages from further edits.	Assist students in archiving their wiki pages, or in sharing the content with their peers or parents.	Students can archive their wiki pages offline, or share them with others.

Further Considerations	
Follow-Up Activities	A follow-up activity might include planning itineraries for a trip to each of the countries students gave their presentations on. Students could be assigned to create a dialog based on that of a travel agent and a client wanting to book a holiday.
Contingency Plan(s)	The next lesson in the course syllabus should be ready in case there is a problem at any stage of wiki development. Alternatively, some language games can be prepared to fill in the time if technological problems occur. Several activity sheets for review of previous material should be prepared to allow those students who complete their scripts or recording to keep busy with language content.
Evaluation	What are the biggest frustrations for implementation? Can these be remedied next time? What are the successes of the lesson? What did students get out of this activity? Can more language practice be provided?

Example Implementation:
Wikis

The Teaching and Learning Context

A wiki can be used for a single class period to review and edit a single paragraph or an entire academic article. Wikis could be applied over a semester or term when working on a more extensive projects or a series of portfolio pieces. The following procedural example presents a ten week outline for the development of article writing and presentation skills, and can be applied with adults over the course of a term in an English for academic purposes (EAP) class in a private institute, college, or university setting.

Teaching Material

When using wikis in the classroom, the teaching material can be broken down into three: the software, the hardware, and the activities or tasks selected as appropriate for the learning context.

The software

Depending on your teaching context, the choice of wiki software will vary. Generally, this comes down to one of two choices either installing wiki software locally and hosting your own wiki, or using existing wiki software that is hosted by a company on the internet. The resources list presents several choices and there should be at least one that potentially offers the best options for your intended use and with which you feel comfortable using with your students. It is likely that this choice will also come down to the ages of your students as well as the teaching locale (for example, grade school, university, or private institute).

The hardware

Depending on how and where the wiki will be accessed by students, a number of different technological requirements regarding hardware will need to be met. If you are working in a bring-your-own-device (BYOD) context, you will need to make sure that the students bring their devices as required and that they have the associated applications installed. If students are using the computers available at school, then the computer lab or computer room may need to be booked. If you are setting wiki use for homework, then you will need to ensure that all students are able to access the hardware required to complete any set wiki work and to use the internet.

The Learning content

A wide variety of tasks and activities are suited to wiki use, and the tasks chosen should take into account the age and maturity levels of learners, their language level, the teaching environment (grade school, university, private institute), and the desired learning outcomes.

Procedure

Wiki use is adaptable to almost any class and learning environment, but their use must be pedagogically sound. The reason for this is that wiki use will see students work together to create knowledge, and develop learning material that is tailored to their learning context. In this regard, individual authorship becomes less important than working collaboratively to successfully complete the outcomes set for the task or project being developed. It is therefore important to regulate and structure the interaction that students have with wikis so that any content produced, edited, and created is completed with these objectives in mind.

Foord (2016) has developed the STOLEN acronym to identify aspects of wiki use that can increase the potential of wikis working well in the classroom context, and for teachers to use as a guide when starting out. This acronym is a useful one to keep in mind when using wikis in any teaching and learning context, and it can be broken down as follows:

- **S**pecific overall objective – set objectives that are clear and understood by all, and this can be guided by providing example pages and templates.
- **T**imely – set time limits and create a wiki with a specific purpose, and with a specific end point to assignments.

- **O**wnership – create ownership in the collaborative wiki space, as this will allow for students to be creative and to make their pages their own.
- Localized objective – establish assignments that allow for familiarization with the wiki at the start as well as the type of use that you envision for it before moving on to more complicated, longer, or bigger tasks.
- Engagement rules – determine who can edit the wiki and to what degree, and develop acceptable and unacceptable guidelines for use.
- Navigation – establish a simple and clear navigational structure this will ensure that wiki content can be easily found and that the structure is easily duplicated by students.

Keep in mind that it is not in and of itself the use of technology that provides learning, but the pedagogy behind it that leads to learning. Careful consideration therefore needs to go into the tasks and activities that students will perform when using a wiki, and how these tasks and activities come to relate to the specific learning outcomes of the course.

Week one – Wiki familiarization

When using a wiki over the course of a term or semester, it is advisable to provide an introduction to the wiki software that will be used, along with some familiarization of what kind of mechanical tasks that students will be expected to perform when using the wiki. This can be achieved by presenting students with a screencast and an associated worksheet so that they can also engage in language learning while becoming familiar with the wiki, and exactly what it is that they will need to be doing with the application throughout the remainder of the course. An overview of the tasks and objectives intended to be achieved by the end of wiki use will also be important to present to students here, so that they can understand why they need to be familiar with wiki use, how it all ties in to their learning goals, and how it can benefit both their language learning and academic skills.

Week two – Editing

Students will need to become familiar with how to edit articles in a wiki environment, and this means being able to understand and use wiki markup language. Again a screencast could be useful here, but perhaps a demonstration and students practicing in the wiki sandbox may be more beneficial. Depending on the objectives of the assignment, you may also want to introduce other factors at this stage to relate the editing process back to the learning objectives and overall outcomes. This could mean going over what constitutes a good article, and how to structure and compose a successful wiki article.

Week three – Exploring the topic

Depending on the topic set for assignment, this week of the course will vary. If you are going to have students explore a topic based on themes that can be expanded into a written article for submission, then one means of exploring the topic might be looking at Wikipedia stubs, and seeing how these topics can be expanded to form a fully developed article. This can also lead into teaching aspects of mind mapping, and how to develop topic outlines when writing. Students can work collaboratively to brainstorm on the topic, and put their ideas in point form or graphic form on the wiki.

Week four – Applying sources

This week of the course could be spent familiarizing students with school policies regarding aspects of copyright and plagiarism. This is important as sometimes determining what is and is not plagiarism can be very difficult for students who are just starting to write more academic style essays. Also being able to write citations correctly in the necessary style of their field of study can also prove to be a challenge. The American Psychological Association (APA), Modern Language Association (MLA), or Harvard referencing styles can then be introduced as a necessary part of academic life.

Week five – Selecting articles

Students need to select a topic, or be provided with a series of choices from the teacher, and begin to find sources that they can reference when constructing their own article. If students are new to the academic setting, this may also prove to be a challenge for them. It may be necessary to teach how to read an abstract, how to identify keywords, how to scan articles, and how to take notes. Sources that students have identified as being useful can then be used as a start in building their bibliography list on the wiki. So too, any sources collated could be used to develop an annotated bibliography with students working on this process either individually or collaboratively.

Week six – Drafting articles

In this week, students begin to write their articles, either editing 'live' or from the sandbox. Students can work collaboratively or individually on developing a summary of what they intend to discuss in their article, fleshing out their previously constructed outlines. The remainder of the writing task can be set as a homework activity, or continued on in the following class sessions.

Week seven – Providing and receiving feedback

After completing a first draft, it is important to get feedback and have fellow students edit other students' articles. It is a good idea to use a checklist for this purpose that can highlight the positives and negatives of the article itself as well as wiki use. Just such a checklist is included in the photocopiable section of this book. Students can also be assigned to look over peer work for grammatical and spelling errors, and to offer suggestions for vocabulary changes and style changes (for example, high modality to low modality).

Week eight – Feedback responses

This week can be used to review the feedback provided by students on others' work, and common problems, mistakes, and errors can be worked through together. This point of the course can also serve as a reminder for students as to what they have achieved and learned so far, and how the wiki is leading to the development of their academic and language skills.

Week nine – Presentations

At this point, all articles have been edited and peer reviewed. They can now be summarized and, along with appropriate media elements, be provided to the class through oral presentations. This can be done individually or collaboratively, with students presenting either their own article or that of other class members. This provides them with the practice in summarizing academic articles that is expected in any academic seminar, and presenting the content in their own words along with an interpretation of their own understanding of the content.

Week ten – Assignment submission

Each stage of article development and culmination in a summary presentation can be graded either as a whole or in part. An appropriate grading scheme would need to be developed, and this would need to cover the outline, the bibliography (annotated or not), the article, and the presentation.

14
Photocopiable material

This section of the book contains all the photocopiable handouts, and you can feel free to make as many copies as you require for teaching purposes and for use within your classes. Any other use or distribution should include a citation to the source of the content.

There are a number of blogs and wikis available on the internet. For a teacher to use these in class would require prescreening to ensure that they are appropriate examples for students to emulate and to determine if they would be suitable for a particular classroom objective or task. Ones which are useful to provide as examples can be gone over with students using the appropriate checklists below. Providing students with these handouts also shows them what is expected of them when they go to complete their own blog posts and wiki articles on assigned topics. This can combine with the handouts on how to write a blog post and wiki article to ensure that students are keeping on track with expectations.

Further, before beginning to use blogs or wikis in the classroom, several considerations will need to be taken into account, and these have been provided for both the teacher and the student. The teacher considerations are holistic, taking into account procedural, technical, pedagogical, and post-pedagogical elements. For students, emphasis on the assignment of specific roles, on top of those expected as part of normal group collaboration, is taken into account, and it reflects the content, resource, and global aspects of writing associated with the construction and refinement of blog posts and wiki articles.

Also provided is a lesson plan template that can be used for considering how best to integrate the steps for using blogs and wikis with your classes. As such, the template is meant to act as means to think about how to implement, with your classes, aspects of what has been discovered through this book. The template should be supplemented with any necessary material, along with the staging as well as other aspects of the lesson being adjusted as required.

The following photocopiable material is available:

- Pre-blog/pre-wiki teacher considerations
- Pre-blog/pre-wiki student considerations
- How to write a blog post resource notes
- How to write a blog post handout
- Peer checklist – Blog post
- How to write a wiki article resource notes
- How to write a wiki article handout
- Peer checklist – Wiki article
- Lesson plan template

Pre-Blog/Pre-Wiki Teacher Considerations

Consider the following elements when utilizing blogs and wikis in the classroom.

Procedural Elements

1. School policies for blog/wiki use have been consulted
2. Parental consent has been obtained where required
3. Students are all aware of safe internet practices

Technical Elements

1. An appropriate blog/wiki tool has been selected
2. Familiarity with site settings for the selected blog/wiki
3. Familiarity with how to post/edit with the selected blog/wiki
4. Settings adjusted on the blog/wiki as appropriate
5. An aggregator has been selected for use

Pedagogical Elements

1. Length of blog/wiki use has been determined
2. Tasks have been selected for use with the blog/wiki
3. Example blog/wiki sites have been selected for introduction
4. Tutorials have been developed to illustrate use
5. Necessary worksheets/handouts have been obtained or developed

Post-pedagogical Elements

1. A means to assess students has been developed
2. The blog/wiki will be locked when showcased

Pre-Blog/Pre-Wiki Student Considerations

All students will help compose and write the blog/posts/wiki articles, and add links or make any associated ongoing edits, comments, and replies. Also, you will need to identify group members who will be responsible for the following roles.

Post/Article Editor(s) _____

1. Keeping the language of the post/article linguistically correct
(e.g. grammar, spelling, vocabulary use)

2. Following writing conventions
(e.g. article flows, correct paragraph structure and formatting)

Citation Editor(s) _____

1. Curating resources

2. Ensuring sources are cited correctly

3. Confirming that all links and media work is as intended

4. Keeping the post/article plagiarism free

5. Maintaining use of copyright free content

Chief Editor(s) _____

1. Ensuring that the layout of the post/article is correct

2. Conducting a final proof of the post/article, tidying up, and correcting errors as necessary

3. Confirming that metadata is accurate, and providing tags

4. Establishing social media links, and the RSS feed

How to Write a Blog Post Resource Notes

Post Title	Group Members
A title is chosen by students.	Student names are listed here.

Topic	Selected by students or provided by teacher.
Target	Students identify target audience, and relevant information regarding their topic.
Post Summary	Students write a short summary of their blog post to ensure that they are covering all details including their stance on the topic (positive or negative, and the reasons).
Post Outline	An outline of the post in point or sentence form needs to be given. Points of research can be added (e.g. links).
Supporting Media	Media choices to support the post need to be included (e.g. links, images, audio, videos, and infographics). All sources are cited.
The Post	The blog post is well composed.
Call to Action	A call to action is included (for example, asking readers to comment, or posing a question for readers to answer in the comments).
Proof, Tidy, Post, and Feed	The post is checked for accuracy (linguistic as well as factual) and appropriateness before it is posted. The post is also search engine optimized (SEO) with tags, working links, keywords, and accurate metadata. An RSS feed is available.

Copyright © David Kent

How to Write a Blog Post Handout

Post Title		Group members	
Topic			
Target			
Post Summary			
Post Outline			
Supporting Media			
Compose			
Proof, Tidy, Post, and Feed			

Photocopiable Content   Copyright © David Kent

Peer Checklist – Blog Post	
Title	☐ Keywords from the post are used
	☐ Written with a hook
	☐ Succinct and focused on topic
Topic	☐ Encourages continued reading
Audience	☐ An intended target audience is identifiable
Post Outline	☐ Headings provide an overview
	☐ Keywords used in sub-headings
Media	☐ Appropriate media used
Post	☐ Responds to task set
Introduction	☐ Succinct and focused on topic
	☐ Key phrases can be used as metadata
Conclusion	☐ Useful, and provides a solution
	☐ Creative and informative
Links	☐ Internal posts ☐ External sites
	☐ Provide relevant/supporting information
Content	☐ Strong, and sums up the post very well
	☐ Call to action included
Comments	☐ Readers can easily leave a comment
Proofing	☐ Plagiarism free ☐ RSS feed included
	☐ No copyright infringement
	☐ Sources cited correctly ☐ Tags added
Requires	☐ Error changes (linguistically/factually)
	☐ More details ☐ Additional evidence
I Have	☐ Posted a comment ☐ Replied to a comment

Copyright © David Kent

How to Write a Wiki Article Resource Notes	
Article Title A title is chosen by students.	**Group Members** Student names are listed here.
Topic	Selected by students or provided by teacher.
Target Audience	Students identify target audience, and relevant information regarding their topic.
Article Summary	Students write a short summary of their article to ensure that they are covering all details, including their stance on the topic (positive or negative, and the reasons).
Article Outline	An outline of the article needs to be given. Points of research can be added (e.g. links).
Supporting Media	Media choices to support the article need to be included (e.g. links, images, audio, videos, and infographics). All sources are cited.
The Article	The article needs to be well composed, and perhaps follow the standard essay structure (introduction, body, conclusion, with attention to paragraph structure – topic sentences, support sentences, and conclusive sentences).
Citations	Citations are included; article is plagiarism free.
Proof, Tidy, Post, and Feed	The article is checked for accuracy (linguistic as well as factual), and appropriateness. The post is also search engine optimized (SEO) with tags, working links, keywords, and accurate metadata. An RSS feed is available.

  Copyright © David Kent

How to Write a Wiki Article Handout	
Article Title	**Group Members**
Topic	
Target	
Article Summary	
Post Outline	
Supporting Media	
The Article	
Citations	
Proof, Tidy, Post, and Feed	

Photocopiable Content   Copyright © David Kent

Peer Checklist – Wiki Article

Title	☐ Keywords from the article are used ☐ Succinct and focused on topic
Topic	☐ Article provides a significant contribution
Audience	☐ An intended target audience is identifiable
Post Outline	☐ Headings provide an overview ☐ Keywords used in sub-headings
Media	☐ Appropriate media used to support article
Introduction	☐ Succinct and focused on topic ☐ Written with a hook
Content	☐ Key phrases can be used as metadata ☐ Responds to task set ☐ Encourages continued reading ☐ Useful and informative
Paragraphs	☐ Contain a single idea ☐ Arguable claims supported ☐ Evidence reflected on
Links	☐ Internal articles ☐ External sites ☐ Provide relevant/supporting information
Conclusion	☐ Strong, and sums up the article
Proofing	☐ Plagiarism free ☐ Sources cited correctly ☐ No copyright infringement ☐ Tags added ☐ RSS feed
I Have	☐ Made error changes ☐ Added details ☐ Provided additional supporting evidence

Photocopiable Content   Copyright © David Kent

Lesson Plan Template	
Teaching Context	
Level of Proficiency and Maturity	
Lesson Length	
Lesson Topic	
Objective	
Outcomes	
Relevant Prior Learning	
Teacher Preparation	
Hardware	
Software	
Webpage Links	
Additional Resources	

Procedure			
Stage and Timing	Objective	Teacher	Students
Review Stage (if required)			
Warm-up Stage/Pre-Technology Use			
Main Stage/ Technology-based Activity			
Practice Stage			
Lesson Summation Stage/Post-Technology Activities			

Photocopiable Content   Copyright © David Kent

Further Considerations	
Follow-Up Activities	
Contingency Plan(s)	
Evaluation	

Photocopiable Content   Copyright © David Kent

15

Resources list

As sites continuously go down, merge, and emerge, perhaps only a small selection of all appropriate resource content should be presented here. An attempt at keeping the number of resources to a select few for each type also provides a sample that is both comprehensive and extensive, but not overwhelming. Like any other instructor resource list, individuals will be able to add to the content as they find material that is useful, creating their own bookmark list, and over time, come to curate a vast resource library tailored to their individual teaching and learning context. Each section of this list is broken down into applications that are mostly all freely available for use with Android or iOS devices, computers, or web-based platforms.

Teachers who wish to make notes, or to record any additional resources that they come across, can use the notes section at the end of this chapter.

The following content is covered:

- App creation
- Audio creation/editing
- Blogs
- Bookmarking
- Books
- Coding
- Comic strip generators
- Copyright
- Digital story creation
- Image resources
- Image editing
- Interactive whiteboards
- Mashups
- Media timelines
- Music resources
- Podcasting
- Podcatchers
- Presentations
- Publishing
- QR codes
- Rubrics
- Screencasting
- Storyboarding and scripting
- Story creation apps
- Video editing
- Video resources
- WebQuests
- Wikis

App Creation

Android – n/a

iOS – n/a

Computer – n/a

Web

Android Creator [free/paid] creates free Android apps without the need for programming knowledge.

AppMakr [free/paid] is a template based application creator that relies on drag and drop of elements for the development of no-coding required applications. It is available in a variety of languages.

Appy Pie [free/paid] relies on templates as well as drag and drop for users to begin creating their app. It requires no coding skills.

AppYourself [paid] is an app creation tool aimed at the business market.

Como DIY [paid] is a do-it-yourself app creation tool aimed to mostly target to businesses, and is available in a number of languages.

iBuildApp [paid] is a template driven app creator for iPhone and Android phones.

Audio Creation/Editing

Android

> *PCM Recorder* [free] is a simple voice recorder.

> *Pocket WavePad* [free] records edits and adds effects to audio.

> *TapeMachine* [paid] is a graphical sound recorder and editor.

iOS

> *Pocket WavePad* [free] records edits and adds effects to audio.

> *Voice Memos* [paid] is voice recorder that allows multitasking.

Computer

> *Audacity* [free] is an open source digital editing program available for Mac and PC which you can use to record, edit and mix narration and music.

> *Pocket WavePad* [free] records, edits, and adds effects to audio for Mac.

GoldWave [free/paid] is a digital audio editor that provides simple recording as well as more sophisticated processing, restoration, enhancement, and conversion for Windows and Linux. A free version is available for evaluation purposes, after which a lifetime license can be purchased.

Web

Twistedwave [free] is a browser-based audio editor that can record or edit any audio file.

Blogs
Android

Blogaway [free] is a simple application to allow blogging on-the-go. It works with Blogger and allows for post creation, adding of photos, videos, multiple account management, saving of drafts, bookmarking, and a host of formatting options.

iOS

Disqus [free] is a commenting system that can be included in blogs as an add-on. The application provides an easy way to moderate comments and publish responses to keep engagement levels high.

TravelPod – Travel Blog [free] is a blogging application that works on- and offline, and is designed to be used while traveling.

Computer – n/a
Web

Blogger.com [free] will host your blog for free, and aside from being very easy to use, it allows some level of privacy so it can be suitable for use as a class blogging site. From a single account, you can create as many blogs as you wish and determine who is allowed to comment on the content.

BuzzSumo [paid] allows users to search for blog posts that have been highly shared across social media.

Edublogs.org [free] allows teachers to create and mange their own and students' websites. There is room for customization of design and the ability to add various media to this private and secure platform.

Kidblog.org [free] is an easy-to-use, safe, and secure publishing platform designed for students in grades K-12. There are a number of excellent features including privacy and password protection, and there is no need for student personal information to be collected, nor is there any advertising. It is free for up to fifty students per class.

WordPress.org [free] is one of the most popular blogging platforms in use today as it is open-source and is easily customizable. The downloadable software for self-hosting purposes is much more flexible than that available on the blogging platform.

Twitter [free] deserves a mention here as it is useful for microblogging (posting short frequent updates). It allows users to post and read short 140-character posts called 'tweets'.

Tumblr [free] is a blogging platform open to those over thirteen years of age, with most users using pen names over their real names when blogging. Users can post on their blog, follow others, and search posts. It is unique in that posts are divided into media types: text, photo, quote, link, chat, audio, and video.

Bookmarking
Android

Bookmark [free] is a cross-platform app that allows for the syncing of bookmarks across different browsers and devices.

Delicious [free] provides users with the ability to organize links to content on the internet that they would like to save, the ability to discover links, edit tags and comments, and also to explore content saved by friends.

Facebook Save [free] is a built-in option for saving Facebook news content to read at a later date.

Instapaper [free] provides an offline archiving solution for web pages, and it presents this content to be read in newspaper fashion. Content can be highlighted, and notes can be added while reading.

Pinterest [free] allows users to pin posts (for example, web pages, images, and videos) and organize them around a common theme.

Pocket [free] integrates with a large number of third party applications that allow for the building of bookmarks. Web pages, videos, images, and whatever else can be used offline for bookmarking. Archiving maintains the links but removes the content from offline availability.

iOS

Delicious [free] allows users to save content from the internet (including web pages, blog posts, tweets, pictures, and video), and provides options for searching through others' collections of links.

Facebook Save [free] is a built-in option for saving Facebook news content to read at a later date.

Instapaper [free] provides an offline archiving solution for web pages and presents this content to be read in newspaper fashion. Content can be highlighted, and notes can be added while reading.

Pinterest [free] allows users to pin posts (for example, web pages, images, and videos) and organize them around a common theme.

Pocket [free] integrates with a large number of third party applications that allow for the building of bookmarks. Web pages, videos, images, and whatever else can be used offline for bookmarking. Archiving maintains the links but removes the content from offline availability.

Computer

EdwinSoft's UltimateDemon [paid] is link building software that helps to provide search engine optimization to a website.

Pinterest [free] allows users to pin posts (for example, web pages, images, and videos) and organize them around a common theme.

Pocket [free] integrates with a large number of third party applications that allow for the building of bookmarks. Web pages, videos, images, and whatever else can be used offline for bookmarking. Archiving maintains the links but removes the content from offline availability.

ReadKit [trial/paid] offers an Apple Mac curative and archiving platform for the content found in your other bookmarking applications (like Pocket and Instapaper) and RSS readers, and provides an extra level of organization to this content.

Web

Delicious [free] is a social bookmarking site that allows users to bookmark webpages to the internet instead of locally.

Facebook Save [free] is a built-in option for saving Facebook news content to read at a later date.

Instapaper [free] provides an offline archiving solution for web pages, and it presents this content to be read in newspaper fashion. Content can be highlighted, and notes can be added while reading.

OnlyWire [paid] works with WordPress and offers automatic submission of content to social networking and social bookmarking sites.

Pocket [free] integrates with a large number of third party applications that allow for the building of bookmarks. Web pages, videos, images, and whatever else can be used offline for bookmarking. Archiving maintains the links but removes the content from offline availability.

Books

Android

Wattpad Free Books [free] provides access to free stories and books written by aspiring authors.

iOS

Free Books – Ultimate Classics Library [free] features free access to 23,469 classic books.

Computer – n/a

Web

BookRix [free] allows access to thousands of books to read either online or to download as ebooks.

Children's Storybooks Online [free] provides a series of illustrated stories for all ages to read.

Coding

Android

Run Marco! [free] offers users the opportunity to play an adventure game while they learn to code. The application presents instructions using 'Blocky', which is the same as that used by the official Hour of Code tutorials.

Tynker [free] is an easy way for children to learn programming skills as they solve puzzles to learn concepts and build games, or control robots and drones. A number of templates are available for free.

iOS

Codea [paid] is a software development tool that uses the Lua programming language to teach users how to program.

Hopscotch [free] is an application that allows users to begin learning to code by making games similar to Angry Birds, and sharing them so others can play them.

ScratchJr [free] allows users to program their own interactive stories and games by snapping together graphical programming blocks. The application was inspired by the Scratch programming language.

Tynker [free] is an easy way for children to learn programming skills as they solve puzzles to learn concepts and build games, or control robots and drones. A number of templates are available for free.

Computer

Scratch [free] allows users to create stories, games, and animations using the Scratch programming language, and then share these with others. It is a project of the Lifelong Kindergarten Group at the MIT Media Lab.

Lightbot – Programming Puzzles [paid] is an OS X game-based application that allows players to use programming logic to solve levels. The app is also available for Android and iOS devices.

Web – n/a

Comic Strip Generators

Android

Comic Maker [free] creates comics from the photo gallery.

Comic Strip It! Lite [free] takes photos or use photo gallery images to create a comic.

iOS

Comic Life 3 [paid] turns photos into comic pages, or creates an entire comic from scratch using templates to build pages with speech balloons, comic lettering, and photo filters.

ToonTastic [free] is a wizard-based animated comic or cartoon creator.

Strip Designer [paid] is software for comic creation that uses camera, library, or Facebook photo options to create a comic.

Computer

Comic Creator [paid] is a basic template driven comic creator for use on a Windows computer.

Web

> *Pixton* [free/paid] is an easy to use comprehensive online comic creator that supports narration, and offers a range of signup options from a free fun option to paid educator/business accounts.
>
> *MakeBeliefsComix* [free] is a basic comic creator that uses black and white images over a four-panel comic strip. An iOS version is also available.
>
> *Toonlet* [free] allows for anyone to create their own cartoon characters and web comics.
>
> *Toondoo* [free] allows for the drag and drop creation of comic strips. An iOS version is also available.

Copyright

Android – n/a

iOS – n/a

Computer – n/a

Web

> *Creative Commons Licenses* [free] gives detailed information regarding the various types of licensing afforded to creative commons, and the permissions that each license grants for the use specific works.

> *Image Codr* [free] can assist learners and teachers alike in determining how a Flickr image can be used (as determined by the original photographer), and provides users with an automatically generated Creative Commons citation regarding the images use within digital projects.

Digital Story Creation

Android

Com-Phone Story Maker [free] combines audio, photos, and text to create stories while allowing for three different layers of audio.

WeVideo [free] is a web-based video editor that can mix images, text, video, and audio.

iOS

30hands [free] creates a story by adding narration to photos.

Magisto [free] uses a wizard to create a short video based on provided images or video content.

Splice [free/paid] combines photos, videos, music and narrations. Effects and transitions can be added.

WeVideo [free] is a web-based video editor that can mix images, text, video, and audio.

Computer

iMovie [paid] provides video creation and editing software that can create easily sharcable content on a Mac. An iOS version is available.

Microsoft Photo Story 3 [free] for Windows lets you create slideshows from a wizard that includes audio, narration, and images.

Windows Movie Maker [free] for Windows operating systems is a video editing software application that allows for narration, audio, images, and video to be mixed and edited, and it comes with transitions and special effects.

Web

Animoto [paid] allows users to submit songs, choose a theme, add their photos, videos, and text to create a digital story that they can share.

Meograph [free] is a digital storytelling tool that relies on Google Earth to create map-based and timeline-based narrated stories.

WeVideo [free] is a web-based video editor that can mix images, text, video, and audio.

Image Resources

Android – n/a

iOS – n/a

Computer – n/a

Web

Cagle Cartoons [free] provides access to a number of political cartoons from around the world. The images are organized by topic with artists categorized by country.

Flickr Creative Commons [free] provides images that can be used for almost any educational project, as long as proper citation is followed

FreeFoto.com [free] has a photos area that is available under three licensing options: recognition, Creative Commons, and commercial.

Morguefile [free] provides a range of images that are copyright free, and are available for use with few or no restrictions.

Pics4Learning.com [free] is a website that provides safe and free images for educational uses. Images here are copyright-friendly and can be used for classrooms, multimedia projects, websites, videos, portfolios, or other projects.

PicSearch [free] allows you to search the internet for images, but be aware that the image may not be copyright-free, or that it may require permission to be used in projects or in any other educational contexts.

The Library of Congress Prints & Photographs Online Catalog [free] makes an attempt to ensure that as many of their images as possible are available online in a digital format.

Wikimedia [free] serves as a point from where all the images and video posted in Wikipedia can be viewed. Most of the images found here are either copyright-free or free for use with minimal restrictions.

Image Editing

Android

PicSay [free] can edit photos, overlay titles, and add special effects.

FX Camera [free] is a photo booth app that allows users to add various effects to photographs.

iOS

PhotoPad [free] can create, edit, and save vector illustrations. It can also work with photo library images.

ScreenChomp [free] allows you to share, explain, and markup images.

Computer

PhotoPad [paid] is an image editor for OS X.

PaintShop Pro [paid] is a comprehensive image editing package for Windows.

Web

Adobe Photoshop CC [paid] is a comprehensive cloud-based image editing package.

Phixr [free] is an online photo editor with various filters and effects, and it can connect to various social media sites.

FotoFlexer [free] is an online image editor offering a number of effects, distortions, and other features.

Pixlr [paid] is a comprehensive online photo editing app.

Interactive Whiteboards

Android

ExplainEverything [free] allows users to share their content by using an interactive screencasting whiteboard.

Interactive Whiteboard [free] is a virtual whiteboard that can be used for drawing or teaching various concepts as it allows for multiple finger input, straight line drawing mode, drawing move mode, and various other features.

PPT and Whiteboard Sharing [free] provides a way to share presentations, videos, and drawings in various settings including the classroom, the boardroom, and online meetings.

Whiteboard: Collaborative Draw [free] is a collaborative drawing application that allows real-time painting.

iOS

Doceri [trial/paid] combines screencasting, desktop control, and an interactive whiteboard in one application, with control through Airplay or through Mac or PC.

Educreations Interactive Whiteboard [free] is an interactive whiteboard and screencasting tool that allows annotation, animation, and narration of a number of content types.

Screenchomp [free] allows users to annotate pictures or to use the application as a whiteboard. Any work completed with the application can be saved automatically to the internet.

ShowMe Interactive Whiteboard [free] allows voice-over recording of whiteboard interactions so that tutorials can be created easily before being shared online.

Computer

Open Sakore [free] is open-source and it is dedicated to teacher and student use. It allows for insertion of multiple document types, along with annotation capabilities for commenting drawing and highlighting content.

Smoothboard Air [free] is a collaborative interactive whiteboard for multiple iPads and for Android tablets. It allows users to annotate desktop applications wirelessly through the use of a web browser.

Web

A Web Whiteboard [free] is a online whiteboard application that allows a number of devices (like computers, tablets, and smartphones), to draw sketches, and to collaborate with others around the globe.

Realtime Board [free] is a whiteboard in a browser that allows for collaboration among a number of users.

Twiddla [free] is a web-based meeting environment that allows users to mark up photos, graphics, and websites, or to just start out with a blank canvas.

Web Whiteboard [free] is a simple way to draw and write together online by creating an online whiteboard with a click, and sharing it live or by sending the link to others.

Mashups

Android

Edjing 5 DJ Music Mixer [free] not only transforms any android device into a turntable, but it provides access to a range of music libraries.

iOS

iMashup [paid] is a professional quality remixing app that allows users to create their own mashups and remixes.

Pacemaker [free] allows users to create and save mixes on an iPhone or iWatch, and to DJ live from iPad devices.

Computer

Mixxx [free] is an advanced open source DJ package that includes an extensive array of features for OS X and Windows.

Web

Mashstix [free] is a website with user submitted mashups available.

Media Timelines

Android

RWT Timelines [free] allows students to create a graphical representation of any event or process by displaying items sequentially along a line. The final product can be exported as a pdf, or saved to the device's camera roll.

Timeline [free] allows users to create timelines and associate them with colors, and to view multiple timelines together. It is a useful reference tool for remembering dates.

iOS

TimelineBuilder [paid] allows users to create custom timelines with images and text with unique beginning and end dates.

Timeline Maker [free] provides an easy way to display a series of events in a chronological order.

Computer

Edraw Timeline Maker [paid] is a tool that makes it simple to create a professional looking timeline, history, schedule, time table, or project plan diagram from scratch.

TimelineMaker [paid] provides a simplified timeline charting tool aimed at project planners, and business professionals, and those in educational contexts.

Web

Capzles [free] allows users to create rich multimedia experiences from videos, photos, music, blogs, and documents by integrating these into a timeline of sequential events, and then share them on various social media platforms.

Hstry [free] is specifically designed for the education sector, and it allows teachers and students to create interactive timelines for assignments and online sharing.

OurStory [free] offers a means for creating story-based timelines with pictures.

Timeline [free] from *readwritethink* allows students of all ages to easily create a graphical representation of related items or events in sequential order and display them along a line using various images and text.

TimeGlider [free] is a web-based timeline project creator that allows zooming and panning across timelines. Users are able to set the size of events as they relate to importance.

Tiki-Toki [free/paid] is a web-based timeline editor that allows viewing of timelines in 3D, and it allows for the integration of images and videos.

WhenInTime [free] is a web application for creating and sharing media-based timelines.

Music Resources

Android

FindSounds [free] can be used to search the internet for sounds that can then be saved as ringtones, notifications, or alarms.

Shazam [free] allows Android device users to identify the music playing around them, as well as discover song lyrics, and other music related information and tracks.

iOS

Shazam [free] allows iOS device users to identify the music playing around them, as well as discover song lyrics, and other music related information and tracks.

Computer – n/a

Web

300 Monks [free] provides a comprehensive source of royalty free music.

ccMixter [free] is a free music site that is community based and promotes a remix culture. *A cappella* and remix tracks licensed under Creative Commons are available for download and use in creative works.

FMA (Free Music Archive) [free] provides access to a range of free music based on a wide variety of genre. The music is offered free under various licenses for use.

Find Sounds [free] is a long-running service that can be used to search the internet for various sounds that can then be incorporated into various projects.

FreePlay Music [free] is a service that searches the internet for free music that can be used in YouTube videos and other projects.

Podcasting

Android

> **Podomatic Podcast & Mix Player** [free] provides access to a wide variety of podcasts, listening in offline mode, and features such as a dynamic social feed so you can see the podcasts Facebook friends follow and like.

iOS

> **PodOmatic Podcast Player** [free] provides access to a wide variety of podcasts, listening in offline mode, and features such as a dynamic social feed so you can see the podcasts Facebook friends follow and like.

Computer

> **Audacity** [free] is a free multi-track audio recorder and editor with some very powerful features that include those for adding effects to files and conducting analysis of the audio recorded.

> **iTunes** [free] offers media on demand and a way to organize and enjoy music, movies, and TV shows, as well as accessing and subscribing to podcasts and screencasts.

LoudBlog [free] is a Content Management System (CMS) for podcasts. This program automatically generates skinnable websites and RSS-feeds for audio and video podcasts, including provision for show notes and links.

PodcastGenerator [free] is an open source content management system for podcast publishing. It provides a comprehensive range of tools to manage all aspects of podcast publishing.

PodProducer [free] allows for the recording of voice and the adding of effects.

Web

ESLPod [free] provides a range of podcast content tailored to second-language learners of English from specific topics through to test-taking guides.

FeedForAll [free] allows for the creation, editing, and publishing of RSS feeds.

Feedity [free] is an online tool for creating an RSS feed for any web page, with an option to upgrade to a premium account that offers additional features.

FETCHRSS: RSS Generator [free] is an online RSS feed generator, that can create a feed out of almost any web page, automatically updates the RSS feed when new content is added to the web page, and generates an RSS for a social networking site.

OPML Viewer [free] allows users to view the contents of outline processor markup language (OPML) files.

Podcast Alley [free] is the place to go if you are interested in podcasts, want to gain access to the top podcasts, and want to find out the latest news about podcasts.

Pod Gallery [free] is a podcasting website where podcasters can share their episodes, and where listeners can subscribe.

QT-ESL Podcasts [free] provides a range of podcasts that cover oral grammar practice and includes scripts and worksheets.

SoundCloud [free] is a social sound platform where anyone is able to create and share audio.

Podcatchers

Android

Podcast Player [free] provides a range of podcast discovery options and tools, along with a range of features including a sleep timer, video support, intelligent silence skip and volume boost, as well as support for tablet, Chromecast, and Android Wear.

Podcast Republic [free] is an application that is ad-supported. It offers a variety of features from podcast discovery and automatic downloading through to storage management, sleep timer, and car mode. Support is also included from Chromecast and Android Wear.

Pocket Casts [paid] shows subscribed podcasts in a tile format, with easy sorting and categorization functions. Video podcast is also supported, along with auto-download and cleanup of downloaded and played episodes to save on storage space. Several features allow it to stand out, including a sleep timer as well as its cross-platform nature that grants it the ability to sync between multiple devices and mobile operating systems.

iOS

Overcast: Podcast Player [free] provides a combination of powerful audio and podcast management features. The application comes with a wide variety of features that allow it to download episodes, send notifications of new episodes, and play content offline or by streaming. It can also normalize speech levels, and speed through gaps and silence in podcasts.

Castro: High Fidelty Podcasts [free] is a simple and easy to use podcatcher. It provides a simple design with automatic episode download, dynamic storage management, along with episode streaming.

Pocket Casts [paid] shows subscribed podcasts in a tile format, with easy sorting and categorization functions. Video podcast is also supported, along with auto-download and cleanup of downloaded and played episodes to save on storage space. Several features allow it to stand out, including a sleep timer as well as its cross-platform nature that grants it the ability to sync between multiple devices and mobile operating systems.

Computer

gPodder [free] is an open source media aggregator and podcast client. It is able to store information in the cloud on which shows you have listened to, and it allows for the local installation of the client for download of content.

iTunes [free] is a comprehensive media aggregator that provides comprehensive support for media management, the audio and video playback of local media, podcast search and subscription, along with automatic downloads, syncing and streaming, and many other features.

Juice [free] is a long-standing cross platform no-frills podcast aggregator that is open source, and specifically designed to manage podcasts. Features include auto cleanup, centralized feed management, and for Windows users, accessibility options for the blind and visually impaired.

Web

Cloud Caster [free] is a web-based podcaster which works across all mobile devices. It syncs progress and playlists across platforms, and provides search and support for audio and video podcasts.

Presentations

Android

Glogster [free] allows students using an Android-based device to create online multimedia posters, or Glogs, from a combination of media types (from audio, graphic, to video), and hyperlinks.

Google Slides [free] allows Android device users with a Google account a means of creating, editing, and collaborating with others on presentations.

LinkedIn SlideShare [free] allows Android device users the ability to search and explore for a variety of presentations, infographics, and documents on topics of their interest.

Microsoft PowerPoint [free] allows users to view PowerPoint presentations on their device for free, and to make edits and changes on the go.

iOS

Glogster [free] allows students using an iOS device to create online multimedia posters, or Glogs, from a combination of media types (from audio, graphic, to video), and hyperlinks.

Google Slides [free] allows iOS device users with a Google account a means of creating, editing, and collaborating with others on presentations.

Keynote [free] is a powerful presentation app that allows users to develop comprehensive presentations with animations, transitions, and multimedia elements.

LinkedIn SlideShare [free] allows iOS device users the ability to search and explore for a variety of presentations, infographics, and documents on topics of their interest.

Microsoft PowerPoint [free] allows users to view PowerPoint presentations on their device for free, and to make edits and changes on the go.

Computer

Microsoft PowerPoint [paid] is a comprehensive presentation software application, and is perhaps the most used and recognizable.

Keynote [free] is a powerful presentation app that allows users to develop comprehensive presentations with animations, transitions, and multimedia elements.

Web

> *Bunkr* [free] is a presentation tool that displays any online content including social media posts, images, videos, audio, articles, and files.
>
> *Glogster* [free] allows students to create online multimedia posters, or Glogs, from a combination of media types (from audio, graphic, to video), and hyperlinks.
>
> *Google Slides* [free] allows those with a Google account, a means of creating, editing, and collaborating with others on presentations.
>
> *LinkedIn SlideShare* [free] allows users to search for presentations, infographics, documents and other items on topics of their interest.
>
> *Microsoft PowerPoint Online* [free] extends the Microsoft PowerPoint experience to the web browser with OneDrive integration, and allows users to create, edit, and view files on the go.
>
> *Prezi* [free] is a visually oriented presentation packaged that also allows users to upload PowerPoint slides, and customize them, or use a variety of their own images, text, audio, and video.

Slidebean [free] offers a one-click presentation development system that incorporates a variety of templates into the design of presentations.

Slides [free] is a place for creating, presenting, and sharing slide decks.

Swipe [free] allows users to share a presentation link with anyone across any device, and it allows viewers to interact with the presentation on several levels, from collaboration through to taking polls.

VoiceThread [free] allows users to import various media such as images, PowerPoints, and PDFs. It provides a means of making audio or video recordings concerning those media artifacts, and it also allows other users to reply to the initial comments, by audio or video means, as the presentation progresses.

Publishing

Android

Book Creator Free [free] offers a simple means of creating a variety of ebooks including picture books, comic and photo books, and journals and textbooks. It allows for the use of images, narration, texts, annotations and drawings.

Book Writer Free [free] is a simple book creation application that allows users to share their content with others.

My Story Builder [free] is a simple, 'suitable for children', book editor.

Scribble: Kids Book Maker [paid] is an application that allows children to write, illustrate, and publish their own comprehensive stories in a range of formations including video export. It contains a series of story starters, stickers, and backgrounds to help them work on creating stories from the start.

iOS

Book Creator Free [free] offers a simple means of creating a variety of ebooks including picture books, comic and photo books, and journals and textbooks. It allows for the use of images, narration, texts, annotations and drawings.

Creative Book Builder [paid] is a professional ebook editor and generator which can also extend the utility of ebooks through the use of a range of widgets.

Demibooks Composer Pro [free] builds interactive books with animation, audio, images, and effects.

Scribble Press – Creative Book Maker for Kids [paid] contains a series of story starters, stickers and backgrounds to help get young kids working on creating stories that can be turned into ebooks.

Computer

Android Book App Maker [paid] provides users with the ability to turn content into a flip-book app.

iBooks Author [free] provides a series of templates and styles to assist in the development of ebooks for the iBook store.

Kotobee [free] provides free software to assist in the creation of ebooks and libraries for a range of platforms.

Web

Blurb [paid] is just one of many online services that can assist in the creation of ebooks.

QR Codes

Android

I-nigma QR & Barcode Scanner (free) is a versatile barcode and QR code reader that can scan a multitude of codes and share these codes as well.

QR Code Reader (free) is a simple QR Code and product barcode scanner.

QR Droid Code Scanner (free) is a powerful barcode, QR code, and Data Matrix scanner that offers multi-language support.

iOS

Bakodo – Barcode Scanner and QR Barcode Reader (free) scans all types of QR codes and barcodes.

QR Reader for iPhone (free) scans a variety of codes including QR codes and barcodes, and features auto-detect scanning.

QRafter – QR Code and Barcode Reader and Generator (free) is a two-dimensional barcode scanner for iOS. Along with a variety of useful features, it can scan and generate QR codes.

Computer

CodeTwo QR Code Desktop Reader (free) allows users to scan QR codes directly from their screen onto their desktop. Users select the QR code to be read by selecting the area with a QR code using their mouse.

QR-Code Studio (free) is for Mac and Windows computers. The QR code maker software is freeware.

Web

QR Code Generator (free) creates QR codes, in a limited number of formats, for free.

QR Stuff QR Code Generator (free) creates QR codes from a various types of data such as website URLs, image files, PDF files, and so on, with static and dynamic embedding options.

The QR Code Generator (free) allows for the free scan and generation of QR codes for a variety of uses.

Rubrics

Android

Daily Rubric: Any Curriculum [free] allows teachers to create and use rubrics from their Android device. Rubrics can be designed from curriculum outcomes, or based on the pre-loaded Common Core Standards.

iOS

Easy Assessment [paid] offers a means to capture and assess performance based on custom created rubrics, scale, or criteria.

Rubrics [paid] allows instructors to track student performance and produce reports based on custom rubrics and grading options.

Computer – n/a

Web

Kathy Shrock's Guide to Everything: Assessment and Rubrics [free] provides access to a wide range of rubrics to help guide assessment of students.

iRubric [free] is a website where instructors can create their own rubrics, or they can build off those made available from other instructors.

RubiStar [free] allows instructors to create their own rubrics using templates designed for core subjects as well as art, music, and multimedia.

Screencasting

Android

AZ Screen Recorder [free] is a screen recording application that offers several features, including the ability to capture the front camera as well as screen recording. It also provides video trimming.

ilos Screen Recorder [free] is a simple application that records the screen and provides audio capture as well.

Telecine [free] is an open source application that allows screen recording through the use of overlays.

iOS

Doceri [trial/paid] combines screencasting, desktop control, and an interactive whiteboard in one application, with control through Airplay or through Mac or PC.

Educreations Interactive Whiteboard [free] is an interactive whiteboard and screencasting tool that allows annotation, animation, and narration of a number of content types.

Screenchomp [free] allows users to annotate pictures or to use the application as a whiteboard. Any work completed with the application can be saved automatically to the internet.

Computer

ilos screen recorder [free] automatically uploads content to their servers for storage and playback.

Screencast-O-Matic [free] offers fifteen minutes of recording time for free, both for screen and webcam, and allows users to save to places such as YouTube or as a video file.

TechSmith Camtasia Studio [free trial] is a comprehensive screen recording application that allows for audio and webcam capture as well as highlighting, adding media, and editing of recordings.

Web – n/a

Storyboarding and Scripting

Android

Ray Story Board [free] is a simple storyboard creator that lets users build storyboards from photos or gallery images, create multiple storyboards, and animate them using a slideshow feature.

Storyboard Studio [paid] is a mobile storyboarding writing tool that is suitable for artists and non-artists alike.

iOS

Penultimate [free] provides a natural feel of writing and sketching on paper, and connects to Evernote.

Storyboard Composer [paid] is a mobile storyboard previsualiztion composer for animators, art directors, film students, film directors, or anyone who would like to visualize their story.

Computer

FrameForge Previz Studio [paid] allows users to develop and previsualize films, TV shows, commercials, or similar projects at a professional level.

Storyboardpro [paid] is professional level software that combines drawing and animation tools with camera controls.

StoryBoard Quick Studio [paid] allows for the fast creation of storyboards with QuickShots, has a print-to-sketch feature, and comes with a series of character poses for integration into storylines.

Web

Google Docs [free] can be used, along with any note-taking or document editor, as a make-shift storyboard by integrating photos or pictures into the document to outline a process or the actions for a story. It is also available as an Android and iOS app.

StoryboardThat [free trial] offers an edition that allows educators to build diagrams, and visualize workflow. It features a drag and drop interface and an extensive image library.

Story Creation Apps

Android

StoryMaker 1 [free] provides a means of creating stories using templates and overlays, and the possibility of using audio, photos, or video.

Storehouse [free] allows users to share a collection of photos in a collage or album, or by telling a story that links the photos.

iOS

StoryKit [free] allows for the creation of an electronic storybook through the use of images, simple drawings, recording of sound, and by the addition of text.

Storyrobe [paid] makes photo-based slideshows with voice recording.

FotoBabble [free] adds audio to a photo to make a talking postcard.

Sock Puppets [free] lets users create lip-synced videos with characters. Various puppets, props, scenery, and backgrounds can be used.

Computer

Cartoon Story Maker 1.1 [free] is a simple program that creates 2D cartoon stories with conversations, dialogs (recorded and/or speech bubble), and various backgrounds.

StoryMaker [free/trial] is game-based software that asks for parts of speech (such as nouns, verbs, adjectives), and these are then inserted into a story with sometimes comical results. Educators can edit and customize aspects of the aspects of the program for their context. Backgrounds can be imported, but character templates are built in.

Web

Littlebirdtales [free] provides younger learners the ability to create digital storybooks.

Pixton [free/paid] is a visual writing tool that allows users to make a comic using images, clipart backgrounds and artwork, as well as speech bubbles.

Storynet.org [free] is a website that aims at connecting people to and through storytelling.

StoryJumper [free] allows users to create illustrated storybooks from scratch or from existing templates.

Video Editing

Android

VideoShow – Video Editor [free] is an all-in-one video editor and slideshow producer that provides music, themes, filters, emojis, as well as text input.

VidTrim [free] is a video editor and organizer that allows the trimming, editing, and saving of videos.

VivaVideo: Free Video Editor [free] is a comprehensive video editor and movie maker that facilitates the creation of video-based stories.

WeVideo [free] is a comprehensive and easy to use video editor that can mix images, text, video, and audio.

iOS

iMovie [paid] is video creation and editing software that can create easily shareable content.

Splice [free] is a video editor that adds music and effects to images and videos with narration. It includes access to free songs, sound effects, text overlays, transitions, filters, and various editing tools.

ReelDirector II [paid] is a full-featured video editing app.

WeVideo [free] is an easy to use and comprehensive video editor that can mix audio, images, text, and audio.

Computer

Windows Movie Maker [free] is a video editing software application that allows for narration, audio, images, and video to be mixed and edited with transitions and special effects.

Web

Video Toolbox [free] is an online video editing and conversion tool.

WeVideo [free] is a comprehensive and easy to use web-based video editor that can mix images, text, video, and audio together to form a compelling story.

Video Resources

Android

TED [free] provides more than 2,000 TED talks from various people by topic and mood, and on a variety of topics.

Vimeo [free] is a variety of videos are available across a wide variety of topics and genres, with users having the ability to upload their own content as well.

YouTube [free] allows for editing and uploading of videos, where one can subscribe to various channels that offer a wide variety of videos on various topics and genres.

iOS

TED [free] provides more than 2,000 TED talks from various people by topic and mood, and on a variety of topics.

Vimeo [free] provides a variety of videos which are available across a wide variety of topics and genres. Users are able to upload their own content as well.

YouTube [free] allows for editing and uploading of videos, where once can subscribe to various channels that offer a wide variety of videos on various topics and genres.

Computer – n/a

Web

Clipcanvas [free] allows for the download of 600,000 royalty free HD and 4K video and film clips.

Mazwai [free] maintains a collection of free to use HD video clips and footage, and some unique time-lapse and slow motion video footages that are provided under the Creative Commons Attribution license if used commercially.

Motion Backgrounds for Free [free] is a place to download professional quality motion backgrounds and video footage.

Motion Elements [free] is a good source for premium stock videos, offering around 400 videos for free, as well as free After Effects templates.

Neo's Clip Archive [free] offers nearly 3,500 free video clips sorted by 25 categories free for use for personal, non-commercial purposes.

Pexels Videos [free] brings under one roof a video library of Creative Commons Zero licensed stock videos from a variety of different sources.

SaveTube [free] allows users to rip YouTube videos to their local computer in various audio or video-based formats.

Savevideo.me [free] allows users to rip videos from a variety of sites to their local computer.

TeacherTube [free] is an online resource that helps users to view and share videos, photos, audio, and documents on almost any topic.

WebQuests

Android – n/a

iOS – n/a

Computer – n/a

Web

Building a WebQuest [free] is a comprehensive overview of the template to follow when there is a need to construct a WebQuest.

Having Fun with Reading [free] is a WebQuest for college and adult level learners of English, where learners interact with texts and complete activities that promote cooperative and collaborative learning along with reading narrative comprehension skills.

Idioms in Your Pocket [free] is a WebQuest that is designed for high school and adult ESL students, and it allows them to discover the various meanings of English idioms.

OneStopEnglish WebQuests [free] provides a selection of WebQuests covering major holidays.

Pre-Writing Your WebQuest [free] provides prompts for users to complete in order to develop a WebQuest.

QuestGarden [free/paid] is a site designed by Bernie Dodge, the creator of WebQuests, for use by pre- and in-service teachers, professional developers, other educators, and those who work with them. The site provides hosting and template creation of WebQuests that then become searchable.

Using WebQuests to Teach English [free] is a WebQuest that can be used to teach teachers about WebQuests.

WebQuestDirect [free] is described as the world's largest searchable directory of WebQuest reviews.

WebQuest.Org [free] provides comprehensive information pertaining to the WebQuest model, and is run by Bernie Dodge, the creator of WebQuests.

Zunal [free/paid] is a site for educators to create, host, and then share their WebQuests with others.

Wikis

Android

EveryWiki: Wikipedia++ [free] aims to provide access to many wikis from a central application.

wikiHow [free] is the application associated with the leading how-to-guide wikiHow. It allows for searching of the wiki to find step-by-step instructions on how to complete almost any task.

iOS

Hack My Life – Life Hack Wiki [free] is an application that seeks to provide access to all possible life hacks. A life hack is a strategy or technique that can be used or adopted to allow for better time management or for getting more out of everyday activities.

Lyrically [free] offers access to a list of song lyrics curated by fans. Searches can be undertaken by track, artist, or by song, and there is support for in-app purchases.

Computer

DokuWiki [free] is a PHP based highly customizable and fully extensible wiki software platform. The advantage is that it requires no databases as all the data is stored in plain text, and for this reason, it is very popular and used by many sites. It has a variety of useful features, from locking to avoid edits through to a spam blacklist.

MediaWiki [free] is open-source and it is the wiki software used by Wikipedia. It is available in a number of languages, released under a general public license (GPL), and written in PHP: Hypertext Preprocessor (PHP) a server-side scripting language. There are many extensions and plugins available for free, including a what-you-see-is-what-you-get (WYSIWYG) editor.

Web

PBworks [free] (formerly PBwiki) is a real-time collaborative editing system with several solutions including one for educators. It offers a single workspace, where student accounts can be created without email addresses, and easy editing without the need for coding.

PmWiki [free] is a wiki tool that gives user-access control over individual pages, so they can be set for access by specific people with it being possible to set different passwords for each page. The software also allows for navigation trails through individual sections, insertion of tables, and provides a printable layout.

Wikidot [free] offers members the ability to create a wiki-based website with forums, where they can create a community, or publish and share documents and content.

Wikispaces [free] is a wiki hosting service that provides educators with a means to monitor student progress in real time and the ability to easily create projects and assign them to students, as well as editing tools and a social newsfeed.

Teacher Notes

Android

_____

_____

_____

_____

_____

_____

_____

_____

_____

_____

_____

_____

_____

_____

_____

_____

_____

_____

_____

_____

_____

_____

iOS

Computer

Web

_____
_____
_____
_____
_____
_____
_____
_____
_____
_____
_____
_____
_____
_____
_____
_____
_____
_____
_____
_____
_____

16
References

Al Khateeb, A. A. (2013). Wikis in EFL writing classes in Saudi Arabia: Identifying instructors' reflections on merits, demerits and implementation. *Teaching English with Technology, 13*(4), 3-22.

Al-Kilidar, H. & Johnson, C. (2009). The use of wikispace in engingeeering education. In *Engineering the Curriculum: Proceedings of the 20th Annual Conference for the Australasian Association for Engineering Education*. December 6-9. Adelaide, Australia.

Aydin, Z., & Yildiz, S. (2014). Using wikis to promote collaborative EFL writing. *Language Learning & Technology, 18*(1), 160-180.

Campbell, A. P. (2003). Weblogs for use with ESL classes. *The Internet TESOL Journal, IX*(2). Retrieved from http://iteslj.org/Techniques/Campbell-Weblogs.html

Foord, D. (2016). Resources – Social software. *A6 Training & Consultancy Ltd*. Retrieved from http://www.a6training.co.uk/resources_Social_Software.php

Gablenick, F., MacGregor, J., Matthews, R., & Smith, B. L. (1990). Learning communitities: Creating connections among students, faculty, and disciplines. New Directions for Teaching and Learning, 41 (Spring). San Francisco, USA: Jossey-Bass.

Gaille, B. (2013). *How many Blogs are on the Internet?* WPVirtuoso. Retrieved from http://www.wpvirtuoso.com/how-many-blogs-are-on-the-internet/

Godwin-Jones, B. Blog and Wikis: Environments for online collaboration. *Language Learning & Technology, 7*(2), 12-16.

Gunelius, S. (2016). What is a blog? *Abouttech*. Retrieved from http://weblogs.about.com/od/startingablog/p/WhatIsABlog.htm

Horvath, J. (2008). Hungarian university students' Blogs in EFL: Shaping language and social connections. *TESL-EJ, 12*(4), 1-9.

James, B. Wide open spaces: Wikis ready or not. EDUCAUSE Review, 39(5), 36, 38, 40, 42, 44-46, 48.

Jatkowski Homuth, J., & Piippo, A. (2012). Using wikis in the ESL classroom. In J. M. Perren, D. Ouano Perren, & T. Dowling (Eds.)., *"Serving for a Better World" Selected Proceedings of the 2012 Michigan Teachers of English to Speakers of Other Languages Conference*. October 12-13, Livonia. Michigan, USA.

Jordan, A., Carlile, O., & Stack, A. (2008). *Approaches to learning: A guide for teachers*. Berkshire: McGraw-Hill, Open University Press.

Keen, A. (2008). *The cult of the amateur: How today's internet is killing our culture*. New York: Nicholas Brealey Publishing.

Kent, D. B. (2015). iPadagogy: Using mobile devices to extend language learning strategies. *The English Connection, 19*(1), 27-30.

Kent, D. B. (2016). Analysis of a Korea-based language teacher organization public social networking service. *International Journal of Contents, 12*(2), 66-74.

Lamb, H. (2004). My brilliant future: Wikis in classrooms. Kairosnews. Retrieved from http://kairosnews.org/node/3794

Leuf, B., & Cunningham, W. (2002). *What is a Wiki.* Retrieved from http://www.wiki.org/ wiki.cgi?WhatIsWiki

Lund, A., & Smordal, O. (2006). Is there space for the teacher in a wiki? *Proceedings of the International Symposium on Wikis,* 37-46.

Mak, B., & Coniam, D. (2008). Using wikis to enhance and develop writing skills among secondary school students in Hong Kong. *System, 36*(3), 437-455.

McLoughlin, C., & Lee, M. W. (2007). Social software and participatory learning: Pedagogical choices with technology affordances in the Web 2.0 era. ICT: Providing choices for learners and learning. *Proceedings ascilite Singapore 2007.* Centre for Educational Development, Nanyang Technological University. December 2-5, Singapore.

Merholz, P. (1999). *PeterMe.com.* Retrieved from https://web.archive.org/web/19991013021124/http:// peterme.com/index.html

Mossberger, K., Tolbert, C. J., & Stansbury, M. (2003). *Virtual inequality: Beyond the digital divide*. USA: Georgetown University Press.

Nassaji, H., & Cummings, A. (2000). What's in a ZPD? A case study of a young ESL student and teacher interacting through dialogue journals. *Language Teaching Research, 4*(2), 95-121.

Nations, D. The Wiki list. *Abouttech*. Retrieved from http://webtrends.about.com/od/wikilists/tp/list_of_wiki_sites.htm

Prensky, M. (2001). Digital natives, digital immigrants. *On the Horizon, 9*(5). Retrieved from http://www.marcprensky.com/writing/Prensky%20-%20Digital%20Natives,%20Digital%20Immigrants%20-%20Part1.pdf

Tinto, V. (2003). Learning better together: The impact of learning communities on Student Success. *Higher Education Monograph Series, 1*.

Vygotsky, L. (1978). Interaction between learning and development. *Mind and Society*. Cambridge, MA: Harvard University Press.

Wortham, J. (2007). After 10 years of blogs, the future's brighter than ever. *Wired*. Retrieved from http://archive.wired.com/entertainment/theweb/news/2007/12/blog_anniversary

Yamauchi, M. (2009). Integrating internet technology into EFL classroom: A case study. *International Journal of Pedagogies and Learning, 5*(2), 3.

Yang, S. H. (2009). Using blogs to enhance critical reflection and community of practice. *Journal of Educational Technology & Society,* 12(2), 11-21.

Yang, C., & Chang, Y. S. (2012). Assessing the effects of interactive blogging on student attitudes towards peer interaction, learning motivation, and academic achievements. *Journal of Computer Assisted Learning, 28*(2) 126-135.

About the Book

Blogs and wikis are different to other websites because they demand interaction. They revolve around information sharing, and allow students to produce content rather than consume it, and react to existing content and influence it. The authorship process gives students a sense of ownership and responsibility to the content that they develop for an audience, as they work together as part of a learning community. They also teach students about personal learning environments, and lend themselves easily to socio-constructivist models of teaching and learning, while providing an avenue for differentiation and the tailoring of instruction to student needs. Throughout this book, the manner in which blogs and wikis are developed is considered while taking into account their pedagogical promise when teaching English to speakers of other languages (TESOL). An overview of instructional strategies, tasks, and activities is provided, along with considerations necessary for applying these tools successfully. Also included are tutorials, photocopiable material, evaluation techniques, and a comprehensive list of resources.

About the Author

David Kent is an Assistant Professor at the Graduate School of TESOL-MALL at Woosong University in the Republic of Korea. He has been working and teaching in Korea since 1995, and with a Doctorate of Education from Curtin University in Australia, he is a specialist in computer assisted language learning (CALL) and the teaching of English to speakers of other languages (TESOL). He has presented at international conferences, as well as published a number of peer-reviewed journal articles, books, and book chapters in his areas of specialization.

Also by David Kent

A Loanword Approach to the Teaching of
English as a Foreign Language in Korea:
Exploring the Effectiveness of a Multimedia Curriculum

Teaching with Technology:
Integrating Technology into the TESOL Classroom

Internet in Education:
Integrating the Internet into the TESOL Classroom

TESOL Strategy Guides
Digital Storytelling
The Prezi Presentation Paradigm
Podcasts and Screencasts
WebQuests
VoiceThreading
Blogs and Wikis

www.ingramcontent.com/pod-product-compliance
Lightning Source LLC
Chambersburg PA
CBHW031544040426
42452CB00006B/176

* 9 7 8 1 9 2 5 5 5 5 1 1 0 *